OLYMPIAD WORKBOOK

INTERNATIONAL ENGLISH OLYMPIAD

01 Learning Objectives

02 Multiple Choice Questions

03 HOTS (Achievers Section)

04 Model Test Paper

05 Answer Keys and Solutions

06 OMR Answer Sheet

V&S PUBLISHERS

Published by:

V&S PUBLISHERS

F-2/16, Ansari road, Daryaganj, New Delhi-110002
☎ 23240026, 23240027 • *Fax:* 011-23240028
✉ info@vspublishers.com • ⊕ www.vspublishers.com

Online Brandstore: amazon.in/vspublishers

Regional Office : Hyderabad
5-1-707/1, Brij Bhawan (Beside Central Bank of India Lane)
Bank Street, Koti, Hyderabad - 500 095
☎ 040-24737290
✉ vspublishershyd@gmail.com

Follow us on:   

BUY OUR BOOKS FROM: AMAZON FLIPKART

© Copyright: *V&S PUBLISHERS*
ISBN 978-81-978021-8-8
New Edition

PUBLISHER'S NOTE

V&S Publishers has carved a significant niche in the publishing industry over the last decade, having successfully published more than 1000 titles across 9 languages spanning over 50 subject categories. Being known for the quality of content, we have built a reputation of excellence and reliability. We have consistently delivered **"Value & Substance"** to our readers, through a wide range of titles across a variety of genres covering school books, fiction and non-fiction that caters to different people from every section of the society.

The **Olympiad Guidebooks for classes 1-10** across all subjects, launched almost a decade ago, under the **GEN X Imprint**, became a go-to-source for the school students in no time, owing to their invaluable and substantive content written in a guidebook pattern,.

Having successfully sold a million copies of the same and in response to demand by both students as well as shopkeepers nationwide; we now present before you our newly launched **Olympiad Workbook Series**, designed for **classes 1-10 across 4 subjects**.

The workbooks are meticulously curated by a team of experienced educators, researchers and subject matter experts, edited by professionals and peer reviewed by teachers. The team has poured its efforts and expertise into creating a crisp and concise workbook which will help and guide the students to the path of success in Olympiad exams. The **MCQs** identified will not only help in scoring top marks in Olympiads but also inculcate a sense of deeper understanding of the subject, by way of solving **HOTS** and referring to complete solutions at the end of the book.

Here we present our new release– **OLYMPIAD WORKBOOK (IEO) CLASS–6** having following features:

☞ Based on the latest syllabi

☞ MCQs with comprehensive coverage of topics

☞ HOTS Questions liberally included

☞ A dedicated chapter on logical reasoning

☞ Model test paper for thorough practice

☞ Sample OMR sheet for real time simulation

We have made sure through our best efforts, that this workbook strictly follows the latest syllabi and patterns of the Olympiad Examination.

As **V&S Publishers** continuously strive to enhance the readability and maintain the credibility of our academic publications, we seek the support of our valuable readers in influencing and enriching the lives of future generations of students.

P.S. While every care has been taken to ensure the correctness of the content, if you come across any error, howsoever minor, do not hesitate to discuss with teachers while pointing that out to us in no uncertain terms.

We wish you all the best for your exams!

DISTINCTIVE FEATURES

01 — Learning Objectives

They list the whole chapter as subtopics, helping the teachers to guide children in a step-by-step manner.

02 — Multiple Choice Questions

MCQs act as an excellent learning aid, helping you to understand and work on your mistakes.

03 — HOTS (Achievers Section)

The High Order Thinking Questions aim to help the student to solve Application-based questions and gain practical understanding of the subject.

04 — Model Test Paper

Model test paper are provided at the end of each book, which help the student to test the knowledge which they have gained after thorough reading of all chapters.

05 — Answer Key

Detailed Answer Key along with explanations aid the pupil to indentify, understand the mistakes they make during the course of Olympiad preparation.

CONTENTS

NOUNS

LEARNING OBJECTIVES

➤ Kinds of Noun
➤ Uses of Nouns

PRACTICE EXERCISE

I. Identify the type of underlined noun(s) in the following sentences and choose the correct option.

1. The <u>plane</u> landed safely at the airport.
   - (A) Proper
   - (B) Common
   - (C) Collective
   - (D) Abstract

2. The <u>paper</u> packages were tied up with strings.
   - (A) Proper
   - (B) Common
   - (C) Collective
   - (D) Abstract

3. <u>Sundarbans</u> is a vast swamp.
   - (A) Proper
   - (B) Common
   - (C) Collective
   - (D) Abstract

4. Our <u>class</u> consists of forty students.
   - (A) Proper
   - (B) Common
   - (C) Collective
   - (D) Abstract

5. She recognized him by his <u>name</u>.
   - (A) Proper
   - (B) Common
   - (C) Collective
   - (D) Abstract

6. <u>Honesty</u> is the best policy.
   - (A) Proper
   - (B) Common
   - (C) Collective
   - (D) Abstract

7. My <u>parents</u> went on a vacation to Las Vegas.
   - (A) Proper
   - (B) Common
   - (C) Collective
   - (D) Abstract

8. <u>Apples</u> are delicious.
   - (A) Proper
   - (B) Common
   - (C) Collective
   - (D) Abstract

9. <u>Zebras</u> and <u>tigers</u> have stripes.
   - (A) Proper
   - (B) Common
   - (C) Collective
   - (D) Abstract

10. <u>Dogs</u> love their families.
    - (A) Proper
    - (B) Common
    - (C) Collective
    - (D) Abstract

11. <u>Cheetahs</u> are man-eating animals.
    - (A) Proper
    - (B) Common
    - (C) Collective
    - (D) Abstract

12. <u>Jason</u> spent more time on Maths.
    - (A) Proper
    - (B) Common
    - (C) Collective
    - (D) Abstract

13. I don't have much <u>luggage</u>.
    - (A) Proper
    - (B) Common
    - (C) Collective
    - (D) Abstract

14. There is room for everyone to sit down; there are a lot of <u>chairs</u>.
    (A) Proper
    (B) Common
    (C) Collective
    (D) Abstract
15. The <u>lioness</u> gave birth to a litter of cubs.
    (A) Proper
    (B) Common
    (C) Collective
    (D) Abstract

II. Identify the type of the underlined noun and choose the correct option.

16. Potato chips are my favourite <u>snack</u>.
    (A) Proper
    (B) Common
    (C) Collective
    (D) Abstract
17. Have you been to the <u>Disney World</u>?
    (A) Proper
    (B) Common
    (C) Collective
    (D) Abstract
18. The museum is closed on <u>Sunday</u>.
    (A) Proper
    (B) Common
    (C) Collective
    (D) Abstract
19. The dog is a <u>faithful</u> animal.
    (A) Proper
    (B) Common
    (C) Collective
    (D) Abstract
20. A <u>herd of cattle</u> was blocking the way.
    (A) Proper
    (B) Common
    (C) Collective
    (D) Abstract
21. I borrowed two books from the <u>library</u>.
    (A) Proper
    (B) Common
    (C) Collective
    (D) Abstract
22. I forgot to carry <u>my pack of cards</u> with me.
    (A) Proper
    (B) Common
    (C) Collective
    (D) Abstract
23. In some countries, people are still not <u>free</u>.
    (A) Proper
    (B) Common
    (C) Collective
    (D) Abstract
24. The <u>Earth</u> is a planet.
    (A) Proper
    (B) Common
    (C) Collective
    (D) Abstract
25. You must always speak the <u>truth</u>.
    (A) Proper
    (B) Common
    (C) Collective
    (D) Abstract

I. **Select the option that identifies noun in the following sentences.**

26. Mr. Dass, have you met your new boss?
    (A) Have   (B) Met
    (C) Your   (D) Boss

27. Her parents tried living in the north, but they could not adapt to the cold.
    (A) North   (B) But
    (C) Not   (D) Adapt

28. Mastering basic mathematics is an important goal for younger students.
    (A) Mastering   (B) Important
    (C) Younger   (D) Students

29. To seize a foreign embassy and its inhabitants is flagrant disregard for diplomatic neutrality.
    (A) Seize
    (B) Its
    (C) Flagrant
    (D) Neutrality

30. The Trojans' rash decision to accept the wooden horse led to their destruction.
    (A) Their
    (B) Led
    (C) Accept
    (D) Destruction

Darken Your Choice with HB Pencil

1.	Ⓐ Ⓑ Ⓒ Ⓓ	7.	Ⓐ Ⓑ Ⓒ Ⓓ	13.	Ⓐ Ⓑ Ⓒ Ⓓ	19	Ⓐ Ⓑ Ⓒ Ⓓ	25.	Ⓐ Ⓑ Ⓒ Ⓓ
2.	Ⓐ Ⓑ Ⓒ Ⓓ	8.	Ⓐ Ⓑ Ⓒ Ⓓ	14.	Ⓐ Ⓑ Ⓒ Ⓓ	20.	Ⓐ Ⓑ Ⓒ Ⓓ	26.	Ⓐ Ⓑ Ⓒ Ⓓ
3.	Ⓐ Ⓑ Ⓒ Ⓓ	9.	Ⓐ Ⓑ Ⓒ Ⓓ	15.	Ⓐ Ⓑ Ⓒ Ⓓ	21.	Ⓐ Ⓑ Ⓒ Ⓓ	27.	Ⓐ Ⓑ Ⓒ Ⓓ
4.	Ⓐ Ⓑ Ⓒ Ⓓ	10.	Ⓐ Ⓑ Ⓒ Ⓓ	16.	Ⓐ Ⓑ Ⓒ Ⓓ	22.	Ⓐ Ⓑ Ⓒ Ⓓ	28.	Ⓐ Ⓑ Ⓒ Ⓓ
5.	Ⓐ Ⓑ Ⓒ Ⓓ	11.	Ⓐ Ⓑ Ⓒ Ⓓ	17.	Ⓐ Ⓑ Ⓒ Ⓓ	23.	Ⓐ Ⓑ Ⓒ Ⓓ	29.	Ⓐ Ⓑ Ⓒ Ⓓ
6.	Ⓐ Ⓑ Ⓒ Ⓓ	12.	Ⓐ Ⓑ Ⓒ Ⓓ	18.	Ⓐ Ⓑ Ⓒ Ⓓ	24.	Ⓐ Ⓑ Ⓒ Ⓓ	30.	Ⓐ Ⓑ Ⓒ Ⓓ

PRONOUNS

LEARNING OBJECTIVES

➤ Basics of Pronoun
➤ Kinds of Pronoun

➤ Uses of Pronoun

PRACTICE EXERCISE

I. **Identify the type of the underlined pronouns and choose the correct option.**

1. <u>She</u> has gone to school.
   (A) Personal   (B) Possessive
   (C) Relative   (D) Reflexive

2. Let me introduce <u>myself</u>. My name is Alan.
   (A) Personal   (B) Possessive
   (C) Relative   (D) Reflexive

3. We need an umbrella. Can you lend us <u>yours</u>?
   (A) Personal   (B) Possessive
   (C) Relative   (D) Reflexive

4. <u>You</u> should be blamed for the mistake.
   (A) Personal   (B) Possessive
   (C) Relative   (D) Reflexive

5. We contributed our share. They have contributed <u>theirs</u>.
   (A) Personal
   (B) Possessive
   (C) Relative
   (D) Reflexive

6. They <u>themselves</u> revealed the truth.
   (A) Personal   (B) Possessive
   (C) Relative   (D) Reflexive

7. This is the girl <u>who</u> spoke to us just now.
   (A) Personal
   (B) Relative
   (C) Possessive
   (D) Reflexive

8. The book <u>which</u> you just bought at the store is a bestseller.
   (A) Personal
   (B) Relative
   (C) Possessive
   (D) Reflexive

9. The baby got up <u>himself</u> after falling down.
   (A) Personal
   (B) Relative
   (C) Reflexive
   (D) Possessive

10. They were looking for a charger. I really don't want to give <u>mine</u> to anyone.
    (A) Personal
    (B) Relative
    (C) Possessive
    (D) Reflexive

11. <u>She</u> prepared the food.
    (A) Personal   (B) Relative
    (C) Possessive   (D) Reflexive

12. We live in an apartment. <u>Theirs</u> is an old-fashioned mansion.
   (A) Personal   (B) Relative
   (C) Possessive   (D) Reflexive
13. Those pet cats are <u>ours</u>.
   (A) Personal
   (B) Relative
   (C) Possessive
   (D) Reflexive
14. <u>You</u> are an angel.
   (A) Personal
   (B) Relative
   (C) Possessive
   (D) Reflexive
15. <u>They</u> are preparing for the examination.
   (A) Personal
   (B) Relative
   (C) Possessive
   (D) Reflexive

II. Choose the correct option to replace the words given in bold.

16. Are these your books? They are not **my books**.
   (A) mine
   (B) ours
   (C) yours
   (D) theirs
17. This is Megha. **Megha** is in my class.
   (A) he
   (B) she
   (C) her
   (D) his
18. My uncle asked me how I managed to find **my uncle's** house.
   (A) he   (B) she
   (C) her   (D) his
19. The speaker used difficult language. No one understood what **the speaker** said

   (A) he
   (B) she
   (C) her
   (D) his
20. I shall mind my business. He should mind my **business**.
   (A) he
   (B) she
   (C) her
   (D) his
21. Teddy's house is right next to **my house**.
   (A) theirs
   (B) mine
   (C) her
   (D) his
22. After Jess got a bad report card, **Jess** wanted to hide it from **Jess's** parents.
   (A) he/his
   (B) she/him
   (C) her/she
   (D) his/him
23. The team is hoping **the team** will regain some of the points they lost in the first round
   (A) he
   (B) she
   (C) them
   (D) they
24. Although Riya started last, **Riya's** was the best looking painting of all.
   (A) he
   (B) she
   (C) hers
   (D) his
25. My clothes were still a little wet when I took **my clothes** out of the dryer.
   (A) them   (B) they
   (C) her   (D) his

26. Identify the sentences in the following questions where pronouns are not needed.
    (A) This is my bag.
    (B) You and I have done our duty.
    (C) One should do ones duty.
    (D) The slave hid himself in a cave.

27. Identify the sentences in the following questions where pronouns are not needed.
    (A) The jury gave its verdict.
    (B) She qualified herself as a doctor.
    (C) They love each other.
    (D) Each will go his own way.

28. Identify the sentences in the following questions where pronouns are not needed.
    (A) Every teacher and every student should do his duty himself.
    (B) That house is ours.
    (C) Give your letter to me.
    (D) I and you have broken this table.

29. Yesterday we entered __I__ new house. It is small but it has all the amenities __II__ a man can dream of. __III__ have named our new house 'The Nest'. Constructing a house is not easy. First, __IV__ has to choose the location then the building plan and then the construction is to be supervised with one's own eyes.

I.	(A) mine	(B) our	
	(C) his	(D) him	
II.	(A) what	(B) which	
	(C) that	(D) his	
III.	(A) His	(B) Him	
	(C) We	(D) Ours	
IV.	(A) oneself	(B) our self	
	(C) myself	(D) one	

1.	Ⓐ Ⓑ Ⓒ Ⓓ	7.	Ⓐ Ⓑ Ⓒ Ⓓ	13.	Ⓐ Ⓑ Ⓒ Ⓓ	19	Ⓐ Ⓑ Ⓒ Ⓓ	25.	Ⓐ Ⓑ Ⓒ Ⓓ
2.	Ⓐ Ⓑ Ⓒ Ⓓ	8.	Ⓐ Ⓑ Ⓒ Ⓓ	14.	Ⓐ Ⓑ Ⓒ Ⓓ	20.	Ⓐ Ⓑ Ⓒ Ⓓ	26.	Ⓐ Ⓑ Ⓒ Ⓓ
3.	Ⓐ Ⓑ Ⓒ Ⓓ	9.	Ⓐ Ⓑ Ⓒ Ⓓ	15.	Ⓐ Ⓑ Ⓒ Ⓓ	21.	Ⓐ Ⓑ Ⓒ Ⓓ	27.	Ⓐ Ⓑ Ⓒ Ⓓ
4.	Ⓐ Ⓑ Ⓒ Ⓓ	10.	Ⓐ Ⓑ Ⓒ Ⓓ	16.	Ⓐ Ⓑ Ⓒ Ⓓ	22.	Ⓐ Ⓑ Ⓒ Ⓓ	28.	Ⓐ Ⓑ Ⓒ Ⓓ
5.	Ⓐ Ⓑ Ⓒ Ⓓ	11.	Ⓐ Ⓑ Ⓒ Ⓓ	17.	Ⓐ Ⓑ Ⓒ Ⓓ	23.	Ⓐ Ⓑ Ⓒ Ⓓ	29.	Ⓐ Ⓑ Ⓒ Ⓓ
6.	Ⓐ Ⓑ Ⓒ Ⓓ	12.	Ⓐ Ⓑ Ⓒ Ⓓ	18.	Ⓐ Ⓑ Ⓒ Ⓓ	24.	Ⓐ Ⓑ Ⓒ Ⓓ		

VERBS AND PHRASAL VERBS 

LEARNING OBJECTIVES

- ➤ Kinds of Verbs
- ➤ Modal verbs and their use
- ➤ Basics of Phrasal verbs
- ➤ Types of Phrasal verbs

PRACTICE EXERCISE

I. Choose the correct option and fill in blanks in the sentences given below.

1. The elephant _________ all over the plants.
   (A) walking   (B) ate
   (C) trampled   (D) sit

2. The pizza _________ slowly in the brick oven.
   (A) cooks   (B) lay
   (C) catches   (D) grew

3. The computer _________ with a loud beep.
   (A) slid   (B) stop
   (C) makes   (D) started

4. I am not _________ to stay out after midnight.
   (A) allow   (B) like
   (C) afraid   (D) go

5. It is time to _________ our meeting for the day.
   (A) started   (B) called
   (C) add   (D) end

6. We _________ the game as a result of our great teamwork.
   (A) won   (B) lose
   (C) loose   (D) win

7. The students _________ to class after recess.
   (A) left   (B) hurry
   (C) take   (D) study

8. Eugene _________ a drum from a big metal can.
   (A) bought   (B) caught
   (C) made   (D) thought

9. Sierra _________ to do her own thing and never to follow the herd.
   (A) likes   (B) try
   (C) proud   (D) makes

10. The loaf of bread began to _________.
    (A) rise   (B) fallen
    (C) decayed   (D) make

II. Choose the correct form of the verb (of being) that best completes each sentence.

11. We _________ seldom as perfect or as accurate as we would like to be.
    (A) is   (B) are
    (C) was   (D) am

12. I _________ hungry now.
    (A) is   (B) are
    (C) was   (D) am

13. A funeral _________ certainly not an opportune time to tell your favourite joke.

(A) was   (B) are
(C) is   (D) am

14. He _________ late yesterday.

(A) is   (B) are
(C) was   (D) am

15. The brown fur of sloths _________ sometimes covered in green algae.

(A) is   (B) are
(C) was   (D) am

III. Choose the correct phrasal verbs to fill in the blanks in the following sentences.

16. I _________ but nobody has seen my wallet.

(A) asked around

(B) asked everyone

(C) asked in

(D) asked out

17. You'll have to run faster than that if you want to _________ with Marty.

(A) catch on

(B) catch up

(C) catch

(D) catch ahead

18. I don't feel like cooking tonight. Let's _________.

(A) eat in

(B) eat along

(C) eat up

(D) eat out

19. I am not being able to _________ his intentions.

(A) figure up   (B) figure out
(C) figure in   (D) figure of

20. The two brothers don't _________ with each other much.

(A) get set

(B) get well

(C) get along

(D) get going

21. The spider taught Robert Bruce to never _________.

(A) give up

(B) give away

(C) give out

(D) give in

22. _________! I'll be there with you soon.

(A) Hang up

(B) Hang there

(C) Hanging

(D) Hang on

23. Sam and Clara's wedding has been _________ for a few days.

(A) called off

(B) given off

(C) set off

(D) put off

24. I am planning to have a _________ at my place soon.

(A) sleep in

(B) sleep over

(C) sleep under

(D) sleep well

25. The twins have _________ their mother more than their father.

(A) taken after

(B) taken to

(C) taken in

(D) taken out

I. Fill in the blanks with correct form of verb.

26. Usually, I _______ parties but I _______ this very much.
    (A) enjoy / am not enjoying
    (B) am enjoying / haven't enjoyed
    (C) enjoy / don't enjoy
    (D) enjoyed / haven't enjoyed

27. It _______ quite often in Britain during the winter.
    (A) is snowing
    (B) snows
    (C) has been snowing
    (D) has snowed

28. Normally, I _______ to bed at around 11.30 every night.
    (A) am going
    (B) have been going
    (C) go
    (D) have gone

II. Choose the correct phrasal verb from the list given below to replace the words underlined and change their form where necessary. There could be an extra phrasal verb:

29. (i) I cannot <u>understand</u> what he says.
    (ii) I <u>met</u> my friend in the park.
    (iii) She failed to <u>appear</u> in time.
    (iv) The strike was <u>withdrawn</u> at last.
    List: take after, call off, make out, turn up, come across.

30 (i) The girl <u>resembles</u> her mother.
    (ii) Evening <u>starts</u> early in winter.
    (iii) Our school <u>closes</u> at 4:30 pm.
    (iv) The school magazine will be <u>published</u> soon.

-Darken Your Choice with HB Pencil-

1. Ⓐ Ⓑ Ⓒ Ⓓ	7. Ⓐ Ⓑ Ⓒ Ⓓ	13. Ⓐ Ⓑ Ⓒ Ⓓ	19 Ⓐ Ⓑ Ⓒ Ⓓ	25. Ⓐ Ⓑ Ⓒ Ⓓ
2. Ⓐ Ⓑ Ⓒ Ⓓ	8. Ⓐ Ⓑ Ⓒ Ⓓ	14. Ⓐ Ⓑ Ⓒ Ⓓ	20. Ⓐ Ⓑ Ⓒ Ⓓ	26. Ⓐ Ⓑ Ⓒ Ⓓ
3. Ⓐ Ⓑ Ⓒ Ⓓ	9. Ⓐ Ⓑ Ⓒ Ⓓ	15. Ⓐ Ⓑ Ⓒ Ⓓ	21. Ⓐ Ⓑ Ⓒ Ⓓ	27. Ⓐ Ⓑ Ⓒ Ⓓ
4. Ⓐ Ⓑ Ⓒ Ⓓ	10. Ⓐ Ⓑ Ⓒ Ⓓ	16. Ⓐ Ⓑ Ⓒ Ⓓ	22. Ⓐ Ⓑ Ⓒ Ⓓ	28. Ⓐ Ⓑ Ⓒ Ⓓ
5. Ⓐ Ⓑ Ⓒ Ⓓ	11. Ⓐ Ⓑ Ⓒ Ⓓ	17. Ⓐ Ⓑ Ⓒ Ⓓ	23. Ⓐ Ⓑ Ⓒ Ⓓ	29. Ⓐ Ⓑ Ⓒ Ⓓ
6. Ⓐ Ⓑ Ⓒ Ⓓ	12. Ⓐ Ⓑ Ⓒ Ⓓ	18. Ⓐ Ⓑ Ⓒ Ⓓ	24. Ⓐ Ⓑ Ⓒ Ⓓ	30. Ⓐ Ⓑ Ⓒ Ⓓ

ADVERBS

LEARNING OBJECTIVES

➤ Basics of Adverbs
➤ Types of Adverbs
➤ Uses of Adverbs

PRACTICE EXERCISE

I. Choose the correct options which the underlined adverbs describe.

1. Thank you for answering my call so quickly.
   (A) call   (B) answering
   (C) you   (D) my

2. Alisha frantically searched for her notebook after working on it many hours the previous night.
   (A) notebook   (B) searched
   (C) working   (D) hours

3. Justin wandered aimlessly through the forest in search of his campsite.
   (A) through   (B) campsite
   (C) forest   (D) wandered

4. After our meal every night, we stroll leisurely in the nearby park.
   (A) meal   (B) park
   (C) stroll   (D) night

5. She sang so heartily that the baby fell asleep.
   (A) sang   (B) baby
   (C) she   (D) asleep

6. He pushed the door forcefully.
   (A) door   (B) he
   (C) pushed   (D) the

7. I vaguely remember my childhood days.
   (A) remember   (B) days
   (C) childhood   (D) my

8. Andrew recently began collecting stamps from various countries.
   (A) collecting   (B) began
   (C) stamps   (D) countries

9. Caleb woke up suddenly when he heard the sound of thunder.
   (A) heard   (B) woke
   (C) sound   (D) thunder

10. He laughed heartily when he heard the funny story.
    (A) heard   (B) story
    (C) funny   (D) laughed

II. Choose the correct adverbs to fill in the blanks.

11. Natalie was sad because she scored _________ on her math test.
   (A) badly   (B) extremely
   (C) nicely   (D) strongly

12. As soon as you are ready, we will _________ leave for the concert.
   (A) obviously
   (B) promptly
   (C) cleverly
   (D) usefully

13. Coming up with new concepts is not easy. Only people who can think ___________ can participate in this contest.
(A) foolishly   (B) lastly
(C) hurriedly   (D) creatively

14. Even after several warnings, Sarah failed to reach on time ___________.
(A) continually   (B) annually
(C) usefully   (D) carefully

15. We will ___________ give up.
(A) never   (B) since
(C) much   (D) very

16. Brenda was sad to go, but she promised to visit ___________ again.
(A) never   (B) soon
(C) only   (D) always

17. ___________ aim high.
(A) early   (B) easily
(C) always   (D) never

18. The maid dropped the vase ___________.
(A) sweetly   (B) carefully
(C) happily   (D) accidentally

19. Olivia's mom ___________ walks to school with her.
(A) angrily   (B) usually
(C) too   (D) softly

20. These boys work ___________ harder than those.
(A) much
(B) very
(C) rarely
(D) never

21. My parents ___________ punished me when they found out that I had cheated on my history test.
(A) happily
(B) proudly
(C) never
(D) immediately

22. He started ___________ but then ran ___________ to finish first.
(A) slowly, quickly
(B) fast, slow
(C) quickly, slowly
(D) slow, fast

III. Choose the correct options to fill in the blanks in the following sentences.

(Hint: Form adverbs by adding "ly" to suitable words. The first one is done for you.)

23. It was really kind of you to help me.
(A) real (correct option)
(B) pure
(C) horrible
(D) faithful

24. She was sleeping so ___________ that she did not want to wake up.
(A) hurry   (B) harm
(C) comfortable   (D) frighten

25. This experiment can go ___________ wrong.
(A) terrible
(B) act
(C) clever
(D) lucky

I. Fill in the blanks with appropriate adverb.

26. They called the police ________ after the accident.

(A) immediately   (B) slowly

(C) peacefully   (D) none of these

27. Kiran is a ______ paid employee of this company.

(A) lowly

(B) highly

(C) hardly

(D) none of these

28. I was stuck in a jam for ________ two hours.

(A) nearly   (B) simply

(C) correctly   (D) none of these

29. How ________ do you go there?

(A) never   (B) seldom

(C) often   (D) none of these

30. Raman was ______ happy when he got his first job.

(A) extremely   (B) fully

(C) halfly   (D) none of these

Darken Your Choice with HB Pencil

1.	Ⓐ Ⓑ Ⓒ Ⓓ	7.	Ⓐ Ⓑ Ⓒ Ⓓ	13.	Ⓐ Ⓑ Ⓒ Ⓓ	19	Ⓐ Ⓑ Ⓒ Ⓓ	25.	Ⓐ Ⓑ Ⓒ Ⓓ
2.	Ⓐ Ⓑ Ⓒ Ⓓ	8.	Ⓐ Ⓑ Ⓒ Ⓓ	14.	Ⓐ Ⓑ Ⓒ Ⓓ	20.	Ⓐ Ⓑ Ⓒ Ⓓ	26.	Ⓐ Ⓑ Ⓒ Ⓓ
3.	Ⓐ Ⓑ Ⓒ Ⓓ	9.	Ⓐ Ⓑ Ⓒ Ⓓ	15.	Ⓐ Ⓑ Ⓒ Ⓓ	21.	Ⓐ Ⓑ Ⓒ Ⓓ	27.	Ⓐ Ⓑ Ⓒ Ⓓ
4.	Ⓐ Ⓑ Ⓒ Ⓓ	10.	Ⓐ Ⓑ Ⓒ Ⓓ	16.	Ⓐ Ⓑ Ⓒ Ⓓ	22.	Ⓐ Ⓑ Ⓒ Ⓓ	28.	Ⓐ Ⓑ Ⓒ Ⓓ
5.	Ⓐ Ⓑ Ⓒ Ⓓ	11.	Ⓐ Ⓑ Ⓒ Ⓓ	17.	Ⓐ Ⓑ Ⓒ Ⓓ	23.	Ⓐ Ⓑ Ⓒ Ⓓ	29.	Ⓐ Ⓑ Ⓒ Ⓓ
6.	Ⓐ Ⓑ Ⓒ Ⓓ	12.	Ⓐ Ⓑ Ⓒ Ⓓ	18.	Ⓐ Ⓑ Ⓒ Ⓓ	24.	Ⓐ Ⓑ Ⓒ Ⓓ	30.	Ⓐ Ⓑ Ⓒ Ⓓ

ADJECTIVES

LEARNING OBJECTIVES

➤ Basics of Adjectives
➤ Kinds of Adjectives

PRACTICE EXERCISE

I. Identify adjectives in the following sentences and choose the correct option.

1. Surprised and excited, Vanessa screamed with happiness when she found her dog.
   (A) Vanessa, dog
   (B) She, her
   (C) Screamed, found
   (D) Surprised, excited

2. The police have found the missing boy.
   (A) missing (B) police
   (C) found (D) have

3. Although it was a cold morning, he did not wear his sweater.
   (A) Although
   (B) morning
   (C) cold
   (D) sweater

4. Aryan lifted the cylindrical beam in the gym.
   (A) cylindrical
   (B) gym
   (C) lifted
   (D) beam

5. The big, black dog chased the tall man.
   (A) big, black, tall (B) big, black, dog
   (C) tall (D) chased

II. Choose the correct descriptive adjectives and fill in the blanks.

6. He was so _________ that he fell asleep as soon as he lay on his bed.
   (A) amused
   (B) frightened
   (C) tired
   (D) clever

7. This sum is too _________ for me to solve.
   (A) difficult
   (B) easy
   (C) many
   (D) simple

8. All the students felt _________ as the teacher was about to announce the results.
   (A) relieved (B) anxious
   (C) angry (D) sorry

9. Everyone applauded Tejas for his ______ act.
   (A) bad (B) mischief
   (C) terrible (D) brave

10. The sky is turning __________ and it seems like it is going to rain.
   (A) red (B) clear
   (C) dark (D) yellow

11. The language of this book is __________ to understand than that one.
   (A) easy   (B) English
   (C) written   (D) French

12. Use your keys to open the __________ door.
   (A) unlocked   (B) locked
   (C) broken   (D) sealed

13. The slope is too __________, you cannot run up it.
   (A) deserted   (B) smooth
   (C) steep   (D) gentle

14. This river hasn't been cleaned since long time. It is very __________.
   (A) muddy   (B) crystal clear
   (C) blue   (D) cold

15. It was __________ of you to offer them help.
   (A) selfish
   (B) horrible
   (C) cruel
   (D) kind

16. I have been feeling __________ lately and have not felt like doing anything.
   (A) energetic
   (B) lazy
   (C) active
   (D) excited

17. Neither Andrew nor Janet likes to talk in front of a __________ group.
   (A) stupid
   (B) clever
   (C) big
   (D) small

18. He draws a __________ salary and leads a __________ life.
   (A) poor, luxurious
   (B) huge, luxurious
   (C) huge, poor
   (D) poor, poor

19. The neighbour's dog was too _____, it would not stop barking at us.
   (A) lovely   (B) friendly
   (C) disciplined   (D) annoying

20. Kevin is __________ because he is going to be a father soon.
   (A) excited   (B) unhappy
   (C) disturbed   (D) heartbroken

III. Find out the type of adjectives of the underlined words and choose the correct option.

21. Seven students did not qualify for the boards.
   (A) Descriptive
   (B) Quantitative
   (C) Demonstrative
   (D) Possessive

22. The bark is the external covering of a tree.
   (A) Descriptive
   (B) Quantitative
   (C) Demonstrative
   (D) Possessive

23. Try using this paintbrush in the art class.
   (A) Descriptive
   (B) Quantitative
   (C) Demonstrative
   (D) Possessive

24. Why didn't you clean your room?
   (A) Descriptive
   (B) Quantitative
   (C) Demonstrative
   (D) Possessive

25. The chameleon can change its color.
   (A) Descriptive
   (B) Quantitative
   (C) Demonstrative
   (D) Possessive

1 Choose the correct adjectival phrase from the options given below:

26. The postman __________ came this morning with a parcel for my mother.
    (A) in his smart uniform
    (B) smart uniformed
    (C) smart uniform
    (D) with his smart uniform

27. While I was walking in the garden, I saw a __________ butterfly.
    (A) coloured brightly
    (B) brightly coloured
    (C) bright colours
    (D) brightly colour

28. I'd like a jar of __________ jam, please.
    (A) home make   (B) home making
    (C) home-made   (D) made home

29. Find out the Adjectives from the following sentences. It is the world's largest group of islands forming a ten thousand islands chain.
    (A) It is the
    (B) world's largest
    (C) group of islands
    (D) a ten thousand islands

30. Find out the Adjectives from the following sentences. Some property of lead is its softness and resistance.
    (A) some property
    (B) lead are
    (C) softness and resistance
    (D) and resistance

Darken Your Choice with HB Pencil

1. Ⓐ Ⓑ Ⓒ Ⓓ	7. Ⓐ Ⓑ Ⓒ Ⓓ	13. Ⓐ Ⓑ Ⓒ Ⓓ	19 Ⓐ Ⓑ Ⓒ Ⓓ	25. Ⓐ Ⓑ Ⓒ Ⓓ
2. Ⓐ Ⓑ Ⓒ Ⓓ	8. Ⓐ Ⓑ Ⓒ Ⓓ	14. Ⓐ Ⓑ Ⓒ Ⓓ	20. Ⓐ Ⓑ Ⓒ Ⓓ	26. Ⓐ Ⓑ Ⓒ Ⓓ
3. Ⓐ Ⓑ Ⓒ Ⓓ	9. Ⓐ Ⓑ Ⓒ Ⓓ	15. Ⓐ Ⓑ Ⓒ Ⓓ	21. Ⓐ Ⓑ Ⓒ Ⓓ	27. Ⓐ Ⓑ Ⓒ Ⓓ
4. Ⓐ Ⓑ Ⓒ Ⓓ	10. Ⓐ Ⓑ Ⓒ Ⓓ	16. Ⓐ Ⓑ Ⓒ Ⓓ	22. Ⓐ Ⓑ Ⓒ Ⓓ	28. Ⓐ Ⓑ Ⓒ Ⓓ
5. Ⓐ Ⓑ Ⓒ Ⓓ	11. Ⓐ Ⓑ Ⓒ Ⓓ	17. Ⓐ Ⓑ Ⓒ Ⓓ	23. Ⓐ Ⓑ Ⓒ Ⓓ	29. Ⓐ Ⓑ Ⓒ Ⓓ
6. Ⓐ Ⓑ Ⓒ Ⓓ	12. Ⓐ Ⓑ Ⓒ Ⓓ	18. Ⓐ Ⓑ Ⓒ Ⓓ	24. Ⓐ Ⓑ Ⓒ Ⓓ	30. Ⓐ Ⓑ Ⓒ Ⓓ

ARTICLES

LEARNING OBJECTIVES

➤ Kind of Articles
➤ Use of Articles

PRACTICE EXERCISE

I. Fill in the blanks with correct article(s) given in the options.

1. _______ Earth revolves around _____ Sun.
   (A) The, the (B) A, a
   (C) An, an (D) None

2. It feels good to perform in front of _______ appreciative audience.
   (A) The (B) A
   (C) An (D) None

3. My eyes hurt. I have to visit _______ eye-doctor.
   (A) The (B) A
   (C) An (D) None

4. Suddenly I heard the whirring sound of _______ helicopter.
   (A) The (B) A
   (C) An (D) None

5. _______ milk comes from cows.
   (A) The (B) A
   (C) An (D) None

6. My father was _______ honest man.
   (A) The
   (B) A
   (C) An
   (D) None

7. Tomorrow evening the whole world will be watching _______ Oscars.
   (A) The (B) A
   (C) An (D) None

8. _______ nightingale is _______ unique bird.
   (A) The, a (B) A, the
   (C) An, a (D) None

9. My favourite subject is _______ Philosophy.
   (A) The (B) A
   (C) An (D) None

10. _______ Dachshund is _______ national dog of Germany.
    (A) The, the
    (B) A, a
    (C) An, an
    (D) None

11. _______ sweeter _______ coffee, _______ better it tastes.
    (A) The, the, the
    (B) A, the, the
    (C) An, a, the
    (D) None

12. _______ water, when heated becomes _______ steam.

(A) The, the
(B) The, none
(C) An, the
(D) None

13. My grandparents lived in _________ one-room apartment.
(A) The
(B) A
(C) An
(D) None

14. _________ price of petrol keeps rising.
(A) The
(B) A
(C) An
(D) None

15. I would like _________ piece of cake.
(A) The
(B) A
(C) An
(D) None

16. Look at _________ woman over there. She is a famous actress.
(A) The
(B) A
(C) An
(D) None

17. _________ computers are useful machines.
(A) The
(B) A
(C) An
(D) None

18. Ben has _________ terrible headache.
(A) The   (B) A
(C) An   (D) None

19. _________ sugar is bad for your teeth.
(A) The
(B) A
(C) An
(D) None

20. Where is _________ book I lent you last week?
(A) The
(B) A
(C) An
(D) None

II. Choose the correct sentence from the given options.

21. (A) India is a democratic country.
(B) The India is a democratic country.
(C) India is the democratic country.
(D) India is democratic country.

22. (A) That is a girl I told you about.
(B) That is girl I told you about.
(C) That is the girl I told you about.
(D) That is an girl I told you about.

23. (A) We reached a hour ago.
(B) We reached an hour ago.
(C) We reached the hour ago.
(D) We reached hour ago.

24. (A) Juan is Spanish.
(B) Juan is the Spanish.
(C) Juan is a Spanish.
(D) Juan is an Spanish.

25. (A) I bought the new TV set yesterday.
(B) I bought an new TV set yesterday.
(C) I bought a new TV set yesterday.
(D) I bought new TV set yesterday.

I. Fill in the blanks with appropriate article.

26. An atheist does not believe in _______ God.
    (A) a   (B) an
    (C) the   (D) none of these

27. He never listens to _______ classical music.
    (A) a   (B) an
    (C) the   (D) none of these

28. You can pay that bill at _______ bank.
    (A) a   (B) an
    (C) the   (D) none of these

29. My flat is on _______ second floor.
    (A) a   (B) an
    (C) the   (D) none of these

30. It was _______ excellent meal last night.
    (A) a   (B) an
    (C) the   (D) none of these

Darken Your Choice with HB Pencil

1. Ⓐ Ⓑ Ⓒ Ⓓ	7. Ⓐ Ⓑ Ⓒ Ⓓ	13. Ⓐ Ⓑ Ⓒ Ⓓ	19 Ⓐ Ⓑ Ⓒ Ⓓ	25. Ⓐ Ⓑ Ⓒ Ⓓ
2. Ⓐ Ⓑ Ⓒ Ⓓ	8. Ⓐ Ⓑ Ⓒ Ⓓ	14. Ⓐ Ⓑ Ⓒ Ⓓ	20. Ⓐ Ⓑ Ⓒ Ⓓ	26. Ⓐ Ⓑ Ⓒ Ⓓ
3. Ⓐ Ⓑ Ⓒ Ⓓ	9. Ⓐ Ⓑ Ⓒ Ⓓ	15. Ⓐ Ⓑ Ⓒ Ⓓ	21. Ⓐ Ⓑ Ⓒ Ⓓ	27. Ⓐ Ⓑ Ⓒ Ⓓ
4. Ⓐ Ⓑ Ⓒ Ⓓ	10. Ⓐ Ⓑ Ⓒ Ⓓ	16. Ⓐ Ⓑ Ⓒ Ⓓ	22. Ⓐ Ⓑ Ⓒ Ⓓ	28. Ⓐ Ⓑ Ⓒ Ⓓ
5. Ⓐ Ⓑ Ⓒ Ⓓ	11. Ⓐ Ⓑ Ⓒ Ⓓ	17. Ⓐ Ⓑ Ⓒ Ⓓ	23. Ⓐ Ⓑ Ⓒ Ⓓ	29. Ⓐ Ⓑ Ⓒ Ⓓ
6. Ⓐ Ⓑ Ⓒ Ⓓ	12. Ⓐ Ⓑ Ⓒ Ⓓ	18. Ⓐ Ⓑ Ⓒ Ⓓ	24. Ⓐ Ⓑ Ⓒ Ⓓ	30. Ⓐ Ⓑ Ⓒ Ⓓ

PREPOSITIONS

LEARNING OBJECTIVES

- ➤ Basics of Preposition
- ➤ Kinds of Preposition
- ➤ Uses of Preposition

PRACTICE EXERCISE

I. Choose the correct options to fill in the blanks with prepositions.

1. He has changed ________ the punishment he received.
   (A) so   (B) to
   (C) from   (D) after

2. The shop remains closed ____________ Sundays.
   (A) on   (B) of
   (C) in   (D) from

3. My father is ________ my returning home late.
   (A) between   (B) against
   (C) before   (D) after

4. He waited for me ________ the station.
   (A) at   (B) about
   (C) down   (D) during

5. There is no point beating ________ the bush.
   (A) on   (B) above
   (C) under   (D) around

6. You should put your family ________ everything else.
   (A) under   (B) before
   (C) after   (D) in

7. I am running ________ schedule.
   (A) behind
   (B) beside
   (C) to
   (D) in

8. I was ________ the flat when the incident took place.
   (A) under   (B) over
   (C) toward   (D) below

9. There is no public holiday ________ May and August.
   (A) in   (B) between
   (C) from   (D) to

10. He passed ________ the park on his way home.
    (A) up   (B) till
    (C) by   (D) near

11. Run ________ quickly and get me some eggs.
    (A) down   (B) over
    (C) in   (D) on

12. It is not good to borrow money ________ anyone.
    (A) off   (B) for
    (C) upon   (D) from

13. There are a lot of clothes stuffed _______ the cupboard.
   (A) on   (B) inside
   (C) outside   (D) over

14. I wanted to talk to you _______ yesterday's quarrel.
   (A) upon   (B) around
   (C) about   (D) amid

15. The teacher asked the students to put _______ their pens.
   (A) on   (B) down
   (C) in   (D) out

16. I am responsible _______ training the new recruits.
   (A) at   (B) about
   (C) with   (D) for

17. I was not quite satisfied _______ the exam results.
   (A) at   (B) for
   (C) with   (D) about

18. Our atmosphere consists_______ oxygen, nitrogen and carbon dioxide.
   (A) into   (B) of
   (C) with   (D) for

19. Diwali is celebrated _______ India in October.
   (A) through   (B) from
   (C) towards   (D) across

20. He got married _______ the age of 28.
   (A) at   (B) in
   (C) on   (D) for

II. Choose the correct option/sentence in each set given below.

21. (A) I didn't have enough money to pay for the meal.
   (B) I didn't have enough money on pay for the meal.
   (C) I didn't have enough money for pay for the meal.
   (D) I didn't have enough money at pay for the meal.

22. (A) Jane goes to the office early in Tuesdays.
   (B) Jane goes to the office early for Tuesdays.
   (C) Jane goes to the office early on Tuesdays.
   (D) Jane goes to the office early upon Tuesdays.

23. (A) Ten people were killed when a bus collided at a car.
   (B) Ten people were killed when a bus collided on a car.
   (C) Ten people were killed when a bus collided towards a car.
   (D) Ten people were killed when a bus collided with a car.

24. (A) I'm dreaming into becoming a famous scientist one day.
   (B) I'm dreaming about becoming a famous scientist one day.
   (C) I'm dreaming for becoming a famous scientist one day.
   (D) I'm dreaming with becoming a famous scientist one day.

25. (A) My cousin is married to a famous actor.
   (B) My cousin is married with a famous actor.
   (C) My cousin is married for a famous actor.
   (D) My cousin is married from a famous actor.

I. **Fill in the blanks with the appropriate preposition.**

26. He congratulated you _______ your promotion.
    (A) in   (B) on
    (C) of   (D) for

27. She jumped _______ the river.
    (A) on   (B) in
    (C) into   (D) to

28. The jug is filled _______ milk.
    (A) of   (B) with
    (C) in   (D) upon

29. My wife is good _______ French.
    (A) in   (B) on
    (C) with   (D) at

30. I am fond _______ reading novel.
    (A) of   (B) by
    (C) on   (D) with

--- Darken Your Choice with HB Pencil ---

1.	(A) (B) (C) (D)	7.	(A) (B) (C) (D)	13.	(A) (B) (C) (D)	19	(A) (B) (C) (D)	25.	(A) (B) (C) (D)
2.	(A) (B) (C) (D)	8.	(A) (B) (C) (D)	14.	(A) (B) (C) (D)	20.	(A) (B) (C) (D)	26.	(A) (B) (C) (D)
3.	(A) (B) (C) (D)	9.	(A) (B) (C) (D)	15.	(A) (B) (C) (D)	21.	(A) (B) (C) (D)	27.	(A) (B) (C) (D)
4.	(A) (B) (C) (D)	10.	(A) (B) (C) (D)	16.	(A) (B) (C) (D)	22.	(A) (B) (C) (D)	28.	(A) (B) (C) (D)
5.	(A) (B) (C) (D)	11.	(A) (B) (C) (D)	17.	(A) (B) (C) (D)	23.	(A) (B) (C) (D)	29.	(A) (B) (C) (D)
6.	(A) (B) (C) (D)	12.	(A) (B) (C) (D)	18.	(A) (B) (C) (D)	24.	(A) (B) (C) (D)	30.	(A) (B) (C) (D)

CONJUNCTIONS

PRACTICE EXERCISE

I. Fill in the blanks with correct options (coordinating conjunction).

1. I was rushing to my appointment, _______ I didn't make it on time.
   (A) and
   (B) so
   (C) for
   (D) yet

2. I got an A in my history test _______ I did well in Maths too.
   (A) and
   (B) nor
   (C) yet
   (D) so

3. I have just eaten dinner _______ I am not hungry.
   (A) and
   (B) or
   (C) so
   (D) but

4. You better hurry _______ you will be late for work.
   (A) and
   (B) or
   (C) so
   (D) but

5. He must be asleep _______ there is no light in his room.
   (A) but
   (B) and
   (C) nor
   (D) for

6. David knew he was wrong, _______ he apologized.
   (A) so
   (B) for
   (C) and
   (D) but

7. I waited for hours _______ she did not come.
   (A) but
   (B) for
   (C) so
   (D) and

8. I am bored. Let's go out for dinner _______ see a movie.
   (A) so
   (B) yet
   (C) and
   (D) but

9. Are you busy this weekend _______ do you have some free time?

(A) and
(B) or
(C) but
(D) for

10. Bela's just got a promotion at work ______________ she is very happy.
(A) and
(B) but
(C) yet
(D) so

II. Fill in the blanks with correct options (subordinating conjunction).

11. ______________ it's raining, I am staying in.
(A) as
(B) when
(C) so that
(D) in case

12. You will succeed ______________ you work hard.
(A) before
(B) until
(C) if
(D) although

13. I don't know ______________ she will come.
(A) after
(B) whether
(C) before
(D) though

14. ______________ she is poor, she is honest.
(A) Since
(B) Because
(C) Though
(D) After

15. ______________ I liked him, I tried to help.
(A) Although
(B) Because
(C) That
(D) Until

16. I will bring my cat ______________ you are allergic.
(A) unless
(B) if
(C) because
(D) since

17. We can travel ______________ land or water.
(A) before
(B) by
(C) so that
(D) when

18. The train had left ______________ we reached the station.
(A) after
(B) since
(C) before
(D) though

19. We haven't had a get-together ______________ you left.
(A) since
(B) even though
(C) although
(D) though

20. Give me something to eat, ______________ I will die of hunger.
(A) unless
(B) else
(C) until
(D) since

I. Fill in the blanks with correct options (correlative conjunction).

21. _____________ Mom _____________ Dad will pick you up.
    (A) Either/or
    (B) Neither/nor
    (C) Both/and
    (D) Not only/but also

22. He is _________ intelligent _____________ good-natured.
    (A) Either/or
    (B) Neither/nor
    (C) Both/and
    (D) Not only/but also

23. _____________ the husband _____________ the wife will be coming.
    (A) Either/or
    (B) Neither/nor
    (C) Both/and
    (D) Not only/but also

24. _____________ the husband _____________ the wife came.
    (A) Either/or
    (B) Neither/nor
    (C) Both/and
    (D) Not only/but also

25. _____________ Alice, _____________ John got the scholarship.
    (A) Either/or
    (B) Neither/nor
    (C) Both/and
    (D) Not only/but also

TENSES

LEARNING OBJECTIVES

- ➤ Basic concepts of Tenses
- ➤ Types of Tenses

PRACTICE EXERCISE

I. **Choose the correct option to fill in the blanks with the correct form of verb.**

1. The plane __________ at 6:30.
   (A) arrives   (B) arrive
   (C) will arrive   (D) arrived

2. Stars __________ brightly in the night sky.
   (A) shines   (B) shining
   (C) shine   (D) will shine

3. Janne__________ eight hours a day.
   (A) work   (B) works
   (C) worked   (D) is working

4. My sister __________ very fast.
   (A) talks   (B) will talk
   (C) is talking   (D) talked

5. My brother and I __________ Japanese.
   (A) speaks   (B) are speaking
   (C) spoke   (D) speak

II. **Choose the correct option to fill in the blanks with the correct form of verb/tense.**

6. Mr. Dan __________ diligently in his factory for five years.
   (A) works   (B) worked
   (C) is working   (D) work

7. He __________ from London yesterday.
   (A) returned   (B) will return
   (C) is returning   (D) returns

8. He __________ ill for a long time.
   (A) has been   (B) had been
   (C) was   (D) is

9. The teacher __________ us a frightening story.
   (A) will tell   (B) is telling
   (C) tells   (D) told

10. I __________ my grandparents last week.
    (A) visit   (B) will visit
    (C) visited   (D) visiting

III. **Choose the correct option to fill in the blanks with the correct form of verb/ future form.**

11. He __________ you tonight after work.
    (A) calls   (B) will call
    (C) is calling   (D) called

12. The children __________ the candy.
    (A) like   (B) liked
    (C) will like   (D) likes

13. Class __________ at 10:30 am.
    (A) will begin   (B) begins
    (C) began   (D) is beginning

14. We are __________ a play at the city centre.
    (A) going to watch   (B) will watch
    (C) watching   (D) watched

15. I _______ you move your things tomorrow.
   (A) help   (B) am helping
   (C) helped   (D) will help

IV. Choose the correct option to fill in the blanks with the correct form of verb/ continuous tense indicated in the bracket.

16. Hurry up! We are _______ for you. (Present)
   (A) waiting   (B) waited
   (C) will wait   (D) wait

17. I _________ all day yesterday. (Past)
   (A) painted   (B) was painting
   (C) will paint   (D) paints

18. He is _________ for Australia. (Present)
   (A) left   (B) will leave
   (C) leaving   (D) had left

19. They _________ the whole time they were together. (Past)
   (A) quarreled
   (B) were quarrelling
   (C) will quarrel
   (D) had quarreled

20. He is always _________ in class. (Present)

   (A) slept
   (B) sleeps
   (C) had been sleeping
   (D) sleeping

21. It happened while I _________ in London last year. (Past)
   (A) lived   (B) had lived
   (C) was living   (D) will live

22. The universe _________ and has been since its beginning. (Present)
   (A) expands   (B) is expanding
   (C) expanded   (D) had expanded

23. The phone rang while I _________ dinner. (Past)
   (A) was having   (B) had
   (C) will have   (D) going to have

24. I _______ letters to my cousins. (Present)
   (A) am writing
   (B) will write
   (C) have written
   (D) wrote

25. The doctor _________ the child. (Past)
   (A) examined   (B) will examine
   (C) had examined (D) was examining

HOTS (ACHIEVERS SECTION)

I. Change the following sentences into negative:

26. Vishal was living in Kolkata in July last year.

27. Vimal was talking to Vijay at ten o'clock last night.

28. At four o'clock yesterday we were all drinking tea.

29. I was trying to get a taxi at ten o clock last night.

30. It was raining in Chennai at five o'clock last evening.

Darken Your Choice with HB Pencil

1. Ⓐ Ⓑ Ⓒ Ⓓ	7. Ⓐ Ⓑ Ⓒ Ⓓ	13. Ⓐ Ⓑ Ⓒ Ⓓ	19 Ⓐ Ⓑ Ⓒ Ⓓ	25. Ⓐ Ⓑ Ⓒ Ⓓ
2. Ⓐ Ⓑ Ⓒ Ⓓ	8. Ⓐ Ⓑ Ⓒ Ⓓ	14. Ⓐ Ⓑ Ⓒ Ⓓ	20. Ⓐ Ⓑ Ⓒ Ⓓ	26. Ⓐ Ⓑ Ⓒ Ⓓ
3. Ⓐ Ⓑ Ⓒ Ⓓ	9. Ⓐ Ⓑ Ⓒ Ⓓ	15. Ⓐ Ⓑ Ⓒ Ⓓ	21. Ⓐ Ⓑ Ⓒ Ⓓ	27. Ⓐ Ⓑ Ⓒ Ⓓ
4. Ⓐ Ⓑ Ⓒ Ⓓ	10. Ⓐ Ⓑ Ⓒ Ⓓ	16. Ⓐ Ⓑ Ⓒ Ⓓ	22. Ⓐ Ⓑ Ⓒ Ⓓ	28. Ⓐ Ⓑ Ⓒ Ⓓ
5. Ⓐ Ⓑ Ⓒ Ⓓ	11. Ⓐ Ⓑ Ⓒ Ⓓ	17. Ⓐ Ⓑ Ⓒ Ⓓ	23. Ⓐ Ⓑ Ⓒ Ⓓ	29. Ⓐ Ⓑ Ⓒ Ⓓ
6. Ⓐ Ⓑ Ⓒ Ⓓ	12. Ⓐ Ⓑ Ⓒ Ⓓ	18. Ⓐ Ⓑ Ⓒ Ⓓ	24. Ⓐ Ⓑ Ⓒ Ⓓ	30. Ⓐ Ⓑ Ⓒ Ⓓ

OLYMPIAD WORKBOOK (IEO) CLASS– 6

VOICE

LEARNING OBJECTIVES

- ➤ Basic concept of Voice
- ➤ Kinds of voice
- ➤ Rules for changing Voice

PRACTICE EXERCISE

I. Choose the sentence which is given in active voice.

1. (A) Beautiful giraffes roam the savannah forest.
   (B) The savannah is roamed by beautiful girraffes.
   (C) The savannahs are roamed by beautiful girraffes.
   (D) None of these

2. (A) Harry ate six pancakes at dinner.
   (B) At dinner, six pancakes were eaten by Harry.
   (C) At dinner, six pancakes are eaten by Harry.
   (D) None of these

3. (A) Sue changed the flat tire.
   (B) The flat tire was changed by Sue.
   (C) The flat tire had changed by Sue.
   (D) None of these

4. (A) A movie is going to be watched by us tonight.
   (B) We are going to watch a movie tonight.
   (C) We are going watch a movie tonight.
   (D) None of these

5. (A) He liked to his students.
   (B) He is liked by his students.
   (C) His students like him.
   (D) None of these

6. (A) I ran the obstacle course in record time.
   (B) The obstacle course was run by me in record time.
   (C) The obstacle course had run by me in record time.
   (D) None of these

7. (A) The entire stretch of highway paved to the crew.
   (B) The entire stretch of highway was paved by the crew.
   (C) The crew paved the entire stretch of highway.
   (D) None of these

8. (A) The novel was read by Mom in one day.
   (B) Mom read the novel in one day.
   (C) Mom has readed the novel in one day.
   (D) None of these

9. (A) He threw the plastic bottles into the crate.
    (B) The plastic bottles were thrown into the crate by him.
    (C) The plastic bottles were thrown in the crate by him.
    (D) None of these

10. (A) The house will be cleaned by me every Saturday.
    (B) I will clean the house every Saturday.
    (C) I will cleaned the house every Saturday.
    (D) None of these

11. (A) She faxed the application for a new job.
    (B) The application for a new job was faxed by her.
    (C) The application for a new job was faxed by her.
    (D) The application for a new job was faxed by her.

12. (A) The entire house was painted by Tom.
    (B) Tom painted the entire house.
    (C) Tom painting the entire house.
    (D) None of these

13. (A) A procession will be hold by them next week.
    (B) A procession will be held by them next week.
    (C) They will hold a procession next week.
    (D) None of these

14. (A) Who taught you to ski?
    (B) By whom were you taught to ski?
    (C) Whom were you taught to ski?
    (D) None of these

15. (A) The whole suburb was destroyed by the forest fire.
    (B) The forest fire destroyed the whole suburb.
    (C) The forest fire destroying the whole suburb.
    (D) None of these

II. Choose the sentence which is given in passive voice.

16. (A) The video was posted on Facebook by Alex.
    (B) Alex posted the video on Facebook.
    (C) Alex has posted the video on Facebook.
    (D) None of these

17. (A) He removed all the evidence.
    (B) All the evidence was removed by him.
    (C) He removed all the evidence.
    (D) None of these

18. (A) You can't blame them.
    (B) They can't be blamed.
    (C) They was't be blamed.
    (D) None of these

19. (A) The team will celebrate their victory tomorrow.
    (B) The victory will be celebrated by the team tomorrow.
    (C) The victory shall be celebrated by the team tomorrow.
    (D) None of these

20. (A) The dishes were washed by John.
    (B) John washed the dishes.
    (C) John wash the dish.
    (D) None of these

21. (A) They were distributing pamphlets.
    (B) Pamphlets is being distributed by them.
    (C) Pamphlets are being distributed by them.
    (D) None of these

22. (A) Larry donated money to the homeless shelter generously.
    (B) Money was generously donated to the homeless shelter by Larry.
    (C) Money were generously donated to the homeless shelter by Larry.
    (D) None of these

23. (A) They occupied the front seats.
    (B) The front seats were occupied by them.
    (C) The front seats was occupied by them.
    (D) None of these

24. (A) The wedding planner will make all the reservations.
   (B) All the reservations will be made by the wedding planner.
   (C) All the reservations shall be made by the wedding planner.
   (D) None of these

25. (A) Susan will bake two dozen cookies for the bake sale.
   (B) For the bake sale, two dozen cookies shall be baked by Susan.
   (C) For the bake sale, two dozen cookies will be baked by Susan.
   (D) None of these

HOTS (ACHIEVERS SECTION)

I. **Choose the correct active/passive voice of the given sentence.**

26. Shivu is singing a song.
   (A) A song has been being sung by Shivu.
   (B) A song is sung by Shivu.
   (C) A song has being sung by Shivu.
   (D) A song is being sung by Shivu.

27. My friends are watching the match.
   (A) The match is watched by my friends.
   (B) The match had being watched by my friends.
   (C) The match is being watched by my friends.
   (D) The match has being watched by my friends.

28. He can speak French.
   (A) French can spoken by him.
   (B) French can be spoke by him.
   (C) French can be spoken by him.
   (D) French could be spoken by him.

29. They may win the battle.
   (A) The battle may be win.
   (B) The battle may be won.
   (C) The battle may be won by them.
   (D) The battle may won.

30. Nobody can catch him.
   (A) He cannot be caught.
   (B) He can not caught.
   (C) He could not be cought.
   (D) He could not cought.

―Darken Your Choice with HB Pencil―

1.	(A) (B) (C) (D)	7.	(A) (B) (C) (D)	13.	(A) (B) (C) (D)	19	(A) (B) (C) (D)	25.	(A) (B) (C) (D)
2.	(A) (B) (C) (D)	8.	(A) (B) (C) (D)	14.	(A) (B) (C) (D)	20.	(A) (B) (C) (D)	26.	(A) (B) (C) (D)
3.	(A) (B) (C) (D)	9.	(A) (B) (C) (D)	15.	(A) (B) (C) (D)	21.	(A) (B) (C) (D)	27.	(A) (B) (C) (D)
4.	(A) (B) (C) (D)	10.	(A) (B) (C) (D)	16.	(A) (B) (C) (D)	22.	(A) (B) (C) (D)	28.	(A) (B) (C) (D)
5.	(A) (B) (C) (D)	11.	(A) (B) (C) (D)	17.	(A) (B) (C) (D)	23.	(A) (B) (C) (D)	29.	(A) (B) (C) (D)
6.	(A) (B) (C) (D)	12.	(A) (B) (C) (D)	18.	(A) (B) (C) (D)	24.	(A) (B) (C) (D)	30.	(A) (B) (C) (D)

NARRATION

LEARNING OBJECTIVES

➤ Concept of Narration
➤ Direct and Indirect Speech

PRACTICE EXERCISE

I. Choose the correct option that expresses direct speech.

1. (A) "He says", I have come to help you.
   (B) He says, I have come to help you.
   (C) "He says, I have come to help you."
   (D) He says, "I have come to help you."

2. (A) The mother said to her son, "Don't go near the fire."
   (B) The mother said to her son, don't go near the fire.
   (C) "The mother said to her son, don't go near the fire."
   (D) The mother said to her son to not go near the fire.

3. (A) Don't waste your money she said.
   (B) "Don't waste your money", she said.
   (C) "Don't waste" your money, she said.
   (D) She said not to waste money.

4. (A) Manu said, I am very busy now.
   (B) "Manu said I am very busy now".
   (C) Manu said, "I am very busy now".
   (D) Manu said he was busy.

5. (A) "Hurry up," she said to us.
   (B) "Hurry up, she said to us."
   (C) Hurry up, she said to us.
   (D) She asked us to hurry up.

6. (A) "Where are you going? James asked Mary."
   (B) Where are you going? James asked Mary.
   (C) "Where are you going?", James asked Mary.
   (D) James asked Mary where she was going.

7. (A) "She said to me, You are my only friend."
   (B) She said to me, You are my only friend.
   (C) She told me I was her only friend.
   (D) She said to me, "You are my only friend."

8. (A) What a lovely place this is! he said.
   (B) "What a lovely place this is! he said."
   (C) He exclaimed this was a lovely place.
   (D) "What a lovely place this is!", he said.

9. (A) "Vote for me and save the country," cried the candidate.
   (B) "Vote for me and save the country, cried the candidate."
   (C) Vote for me and save the country, cried the candidate.
   (D) The candidate asked everyone to vote for him and save the country.

10. (A) He said, I have got a toothache.
    (B) He said, "I have got a toothache".
    (C) "He said, I have got a toothache".
    (D) He said he had a toochache.

II. Choose the correct option that expresses indirect speech.

11. (A) He asked her to give him a cup of water.
    (B) "Give me a cup of water," he told her.
    (C) He asked her to give me a cup of water.
    (D) He asked her to "give him a cup of water."

12. (A) She said to me, "Thank you"
    (B) She thanked me.
    (C) She "thanked me".
    (D) She said thank you.

13. (A) He said that "he had passed the history test."
    (B) He said, "I have passed the history test."
    (C) He said that I have passed the history test.
    (D) He said that he had passed the history test.

14. (A) She requested them not to litter there.
    (B) She requested them "not to litter there."
    (C) She requested do not litter here.
    (D) She politely asked them, "Do not litter here."

15. (A) Rahul asked me, "Did you see the cricket match on TV last night?"
    (B) Rahul asked me if I had seen the cricket match on TV the previous night.
    (C) Rahul asked me did I see the cricket match on TV last night.
    (D) Rahul asked me did you see the cricket match on TV last night.

16. (A) James told his mother that he was leaving for New York the next day.
    (B) James told his mother I am leaving for New York tomorrow.
    (C) James said to his mother, "I am leaving for New York tomorrow."
    (D) James told his mother I am leaving for New York the next day.

17. (A) I said to him, "Why don't you work hard?"
    (B) I asked him why he didn't work hard.
    (C) I asked him why didn't you work hard.
    (D) I asked him why he don't you work hard?

18. (A) He said to her, "What a hot day!"
    (B) He told her what a hot day.
    (C) He exclaimed that it was a hot day.
    (D) He exclaimed to her what a hot day.

19. (A) The priest urged them to be quiet and to listen to his words.
    (B) The priest said, "Be quiet and listen to my words."
    (C) The priest said to them to be quiet and listen to my words.
    (D) The priest said them to be quiet and listen to his words.

20. (A) He asked me how you arrived at the conclusion.
    (B) He asked me, "how I arrived at the conclusion."
    (C) He asked me how did I conclude this?
    (D) He asked me how I arrived at the conclusion.

I. Choose the correct indirect speech of the given sentences.

21. Robin will say to me, "I am your class-mate".
    (A) Robin will tell me that he is my classmate.
    (B) Robin will tell me that he was my classmate.
    (C) Robin will tell me that he will be my classmate.
    (D) Robin said me that he is my classmate.

22. Deepak said to me, "I had finished the coffee."
    (A) Deepak told me that he had finished the coffee.
    (B) Deepak told me that he had been finished the coffee.
    (C) Deepak told me that he had finish the coffee.
    (D) Deepak told me that he finished the coffee.

23. Rahul said to me, " I had gone through it."
    (A) Rahul told me that he have went through it.
    (B) Rahul told me that he have gone through it.
    (C) Rahul told me that he had went through it.
    (D) Rahul told me that he had gone through it.

24. Balaji said to me, "I had been working on it for 5 days."
    (A) Balaji told me that he had been working on it for 5 days.
    (B) Balaji told me that he has been working on it for 5 days.
    (C) Balaji told me that he had worked on it for 5 days.
    (D) Balaji told me that he was working on it for 5 days.

25. Sweety said to me, "I had been writing an essay for 3 hours."
    (A) Sweety told me that she has been writing an essay for 3 hours.
    (B) Sweety told me that she had been writing an essay for 3 hours.
    (C) Sweety told me that she was writing an essay for 3 hours.
    (D) Sweety told me that she had written an essay for 3 hours.

Darken Your Choice with HB Pencil

	A B C D		A B C D		A B C D		A B C D		A B C D
1.	Ⓐ Ⓑ Ⓒ Ⓓ	6.	Ⓐ Ⓑ Ⓒ Ⓓ	11.	Ⓐ Ⓑ Ⓒ Ⓓ	16	Ⓐ Ⓑ Ⓒ Ⓓ	21.	Ⓐ Ⓑ Ⓒ Ⓓ
2.	Ⓐ Ⓑ Ⓒ Ⓓ	7.	Ⓐ Ⓑ Ⓒ Ⓓ	12.	Ⓐ Ⓑ Ⓒ Ⓓ	17.	Ⓐ Ⓑ Ⓒ Ⓓ	22.	Ⓐ Ⓑ Ⓒ Ⓓ
3.	Ⓐ Ⓑ Ⓒ Ⓓ	8.	Ⓐ Ⓑ Ⓒ Ⓓ	13.	Ⓐ Ⓑ Ⓒ Ⓓ	18.	Ⓐ Ⓑ Ⓒ Ⓓ	23.	Ⓐ Ⓑ Ⓒ Ⓓ
4.	Ⓐ Ⓑ Ⓒ Ⓓ	9.	Ⓐ Ⓑ Ⓒ Ⓓ	14.	Ⓐ Ⓑ Ⓒ Ⓓ	19.	Ⓐ Ⓑ Ⓒ Ⓓ	24.	Ⓐ Ⓑ Ⓒ Ⓓ
5.	Ⓐ Ⓑ Ⓒ Ⓓ	10.	Ⓐ Ⓑ Ⓒ Ⓓ	15.	Ⓐ Ⓑ Ⓒ Ⓓ	20.	Ⓐ Ⓑ Ⓒ Ⓓ	25.	Ⓐ Ⓑ Ⓒ Ⓓ

SYNONYMS AND ANTONYMS 

LEARNING OBJECTIVES

➤ Synonyms
➤ Antonyms

PRACTICE EXERCISE

1. DIRECTIONS: Pick out the nearest correct meaning or synonym of the word given below:
   COURAGEOUS
   (A) Fickle
   (B) Insipid
   (C) Timorous
   (D) Fearless

2. DIRECTIONS: Pick out the nearest correct meaning or synonym of the word given below:
   WATCHFULNESS
   (A) Supervision
   (B) Custody
   (C) Superintendence
   (D) Vigil

3. DIRECTIONS: Pick out the nearest correct meaning or synonym of the word given below:
   UNLAWFUL
   (A) Elicit
   (B) Draw
   (C) Egitimate
   (D) Illicit

4. DIRECTIONS: Pick out the nearest correct meaning or synonym of the word given below:
   ATTACHMENT
   (A) Affinity
   (B) Influence
   (C) Causation
   (D) Appendage

5. DIRECTIONS: Pick out the nearest correct meaning or synonym of the word given below:
   WEARY
   (A) Energized
   (B) Fatigued
   (C) Sentimental
   (D) Emotional

6. DIRECTIONS: Pick out the nearest correct meaning or synonym of the word given below:
   BRAVERY
   (A) Onslaught
   (B) Arrogant
   (C) Fortitude
   (D) Nepotism

7. DIRECTIONS: Pick out the nearest correct meaning or synonym of the word given below:
   JEALOUS
   (A) Obvious
   (B) Atrocious
   (C) Envious
   (D) Ferocious

8. DIRECTIONS: Pick out the nearest correct meaning or synonym of the word given below:
   FOUND
   (A) See
   (B) Establish
   (C) Realize
   (D) Search

9. DIRECTIONS: Pick out the nearest correct meaning or synonym of the word given below:
   ALMS
   (A) Blessings
   (B) Charity
   (C) Prayers
   (D) Worship

10. DIRECTIONS: Pick out the nearest correct meaning or synonym of the word given below:

DISCOMFIT

(A) Litigate   (B) Ease
(C) Conflict   (D) Frustrate

11. DIRECTIONS: Pick out the nearest correct meaning or synonym of the word given below:

WRATH

(A) Violence   (B) Anger
(C) Hatred   (D) Displeasing

12. DIRECTIONS: Pick out the nearest correct meaning or synonym of the word given below:

ABSTINENCE

(A) Synchronic   (B) Torrential
(C) Restraint   (D) Gluttony

13. DIRECTIONS: Pick out the nearest correct meaning or synonym of the word given below:

FACULTY

(A) Privilege   (B) Desire
(C) Branch   (D) Ability

14. DIRECTIONS: Pick out the nearest correct meaning or synonym of the word given below:

CHASTE

(A) Filthy   (B) Lewd
(C) Immoral   (D) Noble

15. DIRECTIONS: Pick out the nearest correct meaning or synonym of the word given below:

INTELLECT

(A) Rationality   (B) Imbecility
(C) Insanity   (D) Reverie

16. DIRECTIONS: Pick out the nearest correct meaning or synonym of the word given below:

OMEN

(A) Augury   (B) Superstition
(C) Imagery   (D) Imagination

17. DIRECTIONS: Pick out the nearest correct meaning or synonym of the word given below:

ANIMATE

(A) Kill   (B) Dead
(C) Energise   (D) Calm

18. DIRECTIONS: Pick out the farthest meaning or antonym of the word given below:

INSULT

(A) Humiliation   (B) Credulity
(C) Degradation   (D) Honour

19. DIRECTIONS: Pick out the farthest meaning or antonym of the word given below:

ORIGIN

(A) Ointment   (B) Detergent
(C) Remnant   (D) Comfort

20. DIRECTIONS: Pick out the farthest meaning or antonym of the word given below:

PROVE

(A) Vapid   (B) Assume
(C) Disincline   (D) Atone

21. DIRECTIONS: Pick out the farthest meaning or antonym of the word given below.

INSTANTLY

(A) Repeatedly   (B) Lately
(C) Gradually   (D) Awkwardly

22. DIRECTIONS: Pick out the farthest meaning or antonym of the word given below.

WORTHY

(A) Unimportant   (B) Valuable
(C) Undeserving   (D) Ugly

23. DIRECTIONS: Pick out the farthest meaning or antonym of the word given below.

PARTICIPATE

(A) Precipitate   (B) Change
(C) Disengage   (D) Boycott

24. DIRECTIONS: Pick out the farthest meaning or antonym of the word given below.
HOLLOW
(A) Filled (B) Solid
(C) Strong (D) Substantial

25. DIRECTIONS: Pick out the farthest meaning or antonym of the word given below.
WILD
(A) Arrogant (B) Humble
(C) Tamed (D) Rude

HOTS (ACHIEVERS SECTION)

26. DIRECTIONS: Pick out the nearest correct meaning or synonym of the word given below:
ADVICE
(A) Council (B) Counsel
(C) Practice (D) Proposal

27. DIRECTIONS: Pick out the nearest correct meaning or synonym of the word given below:
QUOTE
(A) Sight (B) Sigh
(C) Sue (D) Cite

28. DIRECTIONS: Pick out the nearest correct meaning or synonym of the word given below:
WISE

(A) Momentous (B) Pragmatic
(C) Judicious (D) Delay

29. DIRECTIONS: Pick out the farthest meaning or antonym of the word given below.
DOMINATE
(A) Defeat (B) Succumb
(C) Threaten (D) Sheepish

30. DIRECTIONS: Pick out the farthest meaning or antonym of the word given below.
INSPIRED
(A) Discouraged (B) Extracted
(C) Negated (D) Admired

Darken Your Choice with HB Pencil

1.	Ⓐ Ⓑ Ⓒ Ⓓ	7.	Ⓐ Ⓑ Ⓒ Ⓓ	13.	Ⓐ Ⓑ Ⓒ Ⓓ	19	Ⓐ Ⓑ Ⓒ Ⓓ	25.	Ⓐ Ⓑ Ⓒ Ⓓ
2.	Ⓐ Ⓑ Ⓒ Ⓓ	8.	Ⓐ Ⓑ Ⓒ Ⓓ	14.	Ⓐ Ⓑ Ⓒ Ⓓ	20.	Ⓐ Ⓑ Ⓒ Ⓓ	26.	Ⓐ Ⓑ Ⓒ Ⓓ
3.	Ⓐ Ⓑ Ⓒ Ⓓ	9.	Ⓐ Ⓑ Ⓒ Ⓓ	15.	Ⓐ Ⓑ Ⓒ Ⓓ	21.	Ⓐ Ⓑ Ⓒ Ⓓ	27.	Ⓐ Ⓑ Ⓒ Ⓓ
4.	Ⓐ Ⓑ Ⓒ Ⓓ	10.	Ⓐ Ⓑ Ⓒ Ⓓ	16.	Ⓐ Ⓑ Ⓒ Ⓓ	22.	Ⓐ Ⓑ Ⓒ Ⓓ	28.	Ⓐ Ⓑ Ⓒ Ⓓ
5.	Ⓐ Ⓑ Ⓒ Ⓓ	11.	Ⓐ Ⓑ Ⓒ Ⓓ	17.	Ⓐ Ⓑ Ⓒ Ⓓ	23.	Ⓐ Ⓑ Ⓒ Ⓓ	29.	Ⓐ Ⓑ Ⓒ Ⓓ
6.	Ⓐ Ⓑ Ⓒ Ⓓ	12.	Ⓐ Ⓑ Ⓒ Ⓓ	18.	Ⓐ Ⓑ Ⓒ Ⓓ	24.	Ⓐ Ⓑ Ⓒ Ⓓ	30.	Ⓐ Ⓑ Ⓒ Ⓓ

WORD POWER

LEARNING OBJECTIVES

➤ Basic concepts of Vocabulary – some everyday problems, relationships, travel and health related

PRACTICE EXERCISE

I. Everyday Problems

Fill in the blanks with the correct option.

1. It is really upsetting when your ____________ because of no fault of yours. It was due to bad traffic.
   (A) miss a flight
   (B) catch a flight
   (C) flight delayed
   (D) reach on time

2. I have sat in office till late every day this week. I feel ________________.
   (A) rested   (B) overslept
   (C) overworked   (D) relaxed

3. In the corporate world, a little bit of healthy ______________ often helps us achieve greater things. But we should stop before it becomes rivalry.
   (A) pollution
   (B) competition
   (C) traffic
   (D) weather

4. ________________ is the urban menace that affects the poor of the society most.
   (A) price rise   (B) excessive heat
   (C) traffic   (D) rainfall

5. I love animals. I would like to work with an organization that fights __________.
   (A) power cut   (B) waterlogging
   (C) competition   (D) animal cruelty

II. Relationships

Fill in the blanks with the correct option.

6. My sister has to travel abroad for work. She wants me look after her two-year-old daughter in her absence. I will be picking up my ________________ on my way home from work today.
   (A) niece   (B) nephew
   (C) sister   (D) cousin

7. Mr and Mrs Reynolds have been like second ______________ to Carrie since she was a child.
   (A) friend   (B) daughter
   (C) son   (D) parents

8. From the time Mahesh has married Pooja, he has been looking after her parents like his own. He is an ideal ______________.
   (A) son
   (B) son-in-law
   (C) nephew
   (D) grandson

9. The best people to tell you about your parent's childhood are your __________.
   (A) grandchildren   (B) son
   (C) grandparents   (D) daughter

10. A female sibling is a __________ and a male sibling is a __________.
    (A) sister/brother   (B) aunt/uncle
    (C) niece/nephew   (D) wife/husband

III. Travel

Fill in the blanks with the correct option.

11. The __________ counter at the airport is where we are supposed to leave our baggage.
    (A) check-in   (B) take-off
    (C) check-out   (D) check-off

12. My house is close to the __________. You can always hear one train or the other chugging past.
    (A) airport   (B) bus stand
    (C) railway station (D) port

13. We start out five-day road trip tomorrow. We must decide which __________ to take before we head out.
    (A) journey   (B) route
    (C) land   (D) trip

14. Have you ever travelled without a ______? I would be scared of getting caught by a ticket-checker.
    (A) suitcase   (B) boarding pass
    (C) passport   (D) ticket

15. You cannot travel abroad without a valid __________.
    (A) passport   (B) luggage
    (C) travel agent   (D) passenger

IV. Health

Fill in the blanks with the correct option.

16. If you have a __________ you must visit the dentist.
    (A) headache   (B) toothache
    (C) stomach ache   (D) heart attack

17. Under a microscope, some __________ appear very beautiful.
    (A) viruses   (B) wounds
    (C) drugs   (D) pill

18. Brent fractured his arm and had to wear a __________ for three weeks.
    (A) pill   (B) operation
    (C) plaster   (D) dose

19. Doctors conduct surgery in the __________. Outside the door of the room, a red light is left on until the procedure is complete.
    (A) operation theatre
    (B) hospital
    (C) pharmacy
    (D) cafeteria

20. If you are feeling __________, you must not go to work. Germs can spread easily.
    (A) well   (B) fit
    (C) healthy   (D) ill

I. Fill in the blanks with correct option.

21. It's time to get rid of the old team and _______ in some fresh ideas.
    (A) set   (B) be
    (C) come   (D) bring

22. I'm very unhappy with the service and I intend to _______ in a complaint.
    (A) cave   (B) take
    (C) dig   (D) put

23. I don't feel we can cope with this and I suggest we _______ in Judith to help us with this.
    (A) come   (B) give
    (C) bring   (D) be

24. The company was in serious financial trouble, so they decided to _______ in the receivers.
    (A) dig
    (B) take
    (C) call
    (D) be

25. It seems a shame to call off the project after all the hard work you have _______ in.
    (A) put
    (B) give
    (C) cave
    (D) dig

Darken Your Choice with HB Pencil

1.	(A) (B) (C) (D)	6.	(A) (B) (C) (D)	11.	(A) (B) (C) (D)	16	(A) (B) (C) (D)	21.	(A) (B) (C) (D)
2.	(A) (B) (C) (D)	7.	(A) (B) (C) (D)	12.	(A) (B) (C) (D)	17.	(A) (B) (C) (D)	22.	(A) (B) (C) (D)
3.	(A) (B) (C) (D)	8.	(A) (B) (C) (D)	13.	(A) (B) (C) (D)	18.	(A) (B) (C) (D)	23.	(A) (B) (C) (D)
4.	(A) (B) (C) (D)	9.	(A) (B) (C) (D)	14.	(A) (B) (C) (D)	19.	(A) (B) (C) (D)	24.	(A) (B) (C) (D)
5.	(A) (B) (C) (D)	10.	(A) (B) (C) (D)	15.	(A) (B) (C) (D)	20.	(A) (B) (C) (D)	25.	(A) (B) (C) (D)

COMPREHENSION

LEARNING OBJECTIVES

➤ Tips for Reading Comprehension

PRACTICE EXERCISE

I. Read the following newspaper headlines and choose the correct option to answer the questions that follow.

1. What is the name of the newspaper in which the article has been published?
   (A) The New York Times
   (B) The Daily Mirror
   (C) The Newark Advocate
   (D) London Herald

2. How many people are killed?
   (A) 868　　　　　(B) 1,341
   (C) 2,200　　　　(D) 1,500

3. Some of the survivors were rescued by…
   (A) Carpathia
   (B) The government
   (C) Sailors
   (D) Family members

4. How many pages does the newspaper have?
   (A) 12
   (B) 5
   (C) 24
   (D) 17

5. Whose family were Titanic passengers?
   (A) Captain of Carpathia
   (B) Someone who works with the newspaper
   (C) A famous actor
   (D) A politician

II. Read the brochure and choose the correct option to answer the questions that follow.

LANGUAGE CENTRE

presents

Talkwell,

a Holiday Camp for Children

Ever paid attention to your child's spoken English? Have you wondered how to improve his or her vocabulary?

Considering how important it is to speak English fluently and with confidence in this competitive world, it is natural for you to worry about your child's command over the English language.

LANGUAGE CENTRE in collaboration with ELLI, the English Language Learning Institute USA presents Talkwell, a fun-filled holiday camp for primary children where they will learn to speak English correctly and fluently.

Taught through interactive games and activities, the training ensures that children learn and practice what they have learnt.

Online applications are welcome. Email: www.langcentre.com

Or or step into any of our centres.

Duration of course: 4 weeks

Last date of application: One week before the beginning of June holidays

6. The camp advertised is to help children to be able to
   (A) read and write English
   (B) speak English correctly and fluently
   (C) score top marks
   (D) impress others

7. The name of the course is
   (A) Talksmart   (B) Talkwell
   (C) Language Centre (D) ELLI

8. What is the duration of the course?
   (A) 3 weeks
   (B) 4 days
   (C) 4 weeks
   (D) 4 months

9. The encourage enrolment, the advertiser offers
   (A) computer-based programmes
   (B) free prizes
   (C) discounts
   (D) free registration

10. What is the full form of ELLI?
    (A) English Language and Literature Institute
    (B) English Learning Language Institute
    (C) English Language Learning Institute
    (D) English Learning Leading Institute

III. **Read the brochure and choose the correct option to answer the questions that follow.**

FREEDOM CARNIVAL
HELIOS THE WATCH STORE
WISHES YOU A HAPPY INDEPENDENCE DAY & INVITES YOU TO
HELIOS END OF SEASON
SALE
UPTO 50 % OFF
ON OVER 25 INTERNATIONAL BRANDS
+
Additional 5% OFF
For first 50 customers
From 13th to 16th August, 2015 at Helios – The Watch Store
Esplanade Crossing: 2nd Block, Park Square Road
Nehru Nagar: 100 Feet Road, Mall Junction
Rajabazar: 3/6 Oberoi Building, Near Music World

11. Why is the company having a sale?
    (A) to celebrate Diwali
    (B) to celebrate Independence Day
    (C) it's the annual sale
    (D) to clear stock

12. Who is going to get an additional 5% off?
    (A) company staff
    (B) previous owners of Helios watches
    (C) first 50 customers
    (D) those who have membership cards

13. What is the name of the sale?
    (A) Freedom Carnival
    (B) Freedom Fest
    (C) Freedom Sale
    (D) Freedom Celebrations
14. For how many days will the sale be on?
    (A) 10 days
    (B) 2 weeks
    (C) whole of August
    (D) 4 days
15. How much discount has been announced?
    (A) 50 %   (B) Up to 50 %
    (C) 25 %   (D) 15 %

IV. Read the itinerary and choose the correct option to answer the questions that follow.

Three Days in Mumbai

Day 1: Kolkata to Mumbai

Travel from Kolkata airport on an Air India flight to Mumbai. On arrival in Mumbai our friendly local representatives will be there to greet you and transfer you to your hotel. Enjoy the rest of the day relaxing.

Day 2: Mumbai Sightseeing

This morning, enjoy the sights of Mumbai on a city tour. Start your Mumbai *darshan* with the Gateway of India – Mumbai's famous monument and the best starting point for tourist to explore the city. Take a drive up the Malabar Hill to the lovely Hanging Gardens and the Kamla Nehru Park. Then experience the wonderful view of Mumbai and the Arabian Sea.

Day 3: Mumbai Markets and Munchies

Mumbai locals love to shop and eat, and with some of the best markets in the country to browse, there's no reason why you shouldn't join in. Whether you're looking for jewellery, saris, antiques or contemporary fashion, you'll find it at one of Mumbai's many markets. When you're feeling hungry after all the hard bargaining, head to Chowpatty Beach at dusk to watch the sunset and snack on Mumbai street food.

Day 4: Harbor and Caves Excursion

What better way to spend your last day in Mumbai than by admiring the port before taking a scenic boat cruise over the waters of Mumbai Harbour. Or ride a ferry over to Elephanta Island, to explore the caverns and the beautiful Hindu temple sculptures of the Elephanta Caves.

16. Which airline are the tourists going to fly through?
    (A) Air India
    (B) Indian Airlines
    (C) Indigo
    (D) Spice Jet
17. What will the tourists see on Day 1?
    (A) the beach
    (B) The Gateway of India
    (C) the harbor
    (D) none of the above
18. Which water body are we close to when we are in Mumbai?
    (A) Indian Ocean   (B) Bay of Bengal
    (C) Arabian Sea   (D) Andaman Sea
19. What do the tourists do on Day 3?
    (A) sightseeing   (B) cruise
    (C) eat and shop   (D) return home
20. How will the tourists reach the Elephanta Island?
    (A) car   (B) ferry
    (C) walk down   (D) bus

V. Read the letter given below and choose the correct option to answer the questions that follow.

G135, 2nd Floor,
Vasant Kunj Apartments
New Delhi 110019

Lifestyle Stores
Vasant Kunj Mall
New Delhi

Dear Sir/Madam,

On March 5, 2010, I bought a Tolke-in Idli Kit from your store at the Vasant Kunj Mall. The cashier who assisted me was Rajesh. He was very friendly and assured me that the Tolke-in Idli Kit would live up to the guarantee on the box and produce perfect idlis each time.

Unfortunately, this product did not live up to its claim. The idlis I made were far from perfect. I followed the directions included in the package very carefully. First, I removed the bag of mix from the box. Then, I poured it into a bowl. Next, I added the correct amount of water to the mix and stirred it. Finally, I poured the mix into the idli tins and kept it in the oven at 350 degrees for exactly 20 minutes.

When the idlis finished cooking, I was very excited to eat them. You can imagine my disappointment when, upon tasting the idlis, I discovered that they were not perfect. These idlis were, in fact, absolutely terrible.

I would appreciate a full refund (Rs 1,500) for this product as soon as possible. Enclosed are the receipt, the empty box, and one of the un-perfect idlis so that you can experience it for yourself. Thank you for your prompt attention to this matter.

Sincerely,

Manoj Saxena

21. This letter is most likely addressed to
    (A) the owner of the idli kit company
    (B) local storeowner
    (C) the clerk at a local idli joint
    (D) Rajesh, the cashier who sold the idli kit

22. The tone of the author can best be described as
    (A) furious   (B) disgusted
    (C) embarrassed   (D) frustrated

23. As used in paragraph 1, which is the best synonym for guarantee?
    (A) lie   (B) warning
    (C) promise   (D) sentence

24. The author is disappointed by the product because
    (A) it was worth less money than he paid for it
    (B) it did not fulfill the promise made on the box
    (C) the directions included with the product contained a mistake
    (D) the directions included with the product were too difficult to follow

25. The author's main purpose in writing this letter is to
    (A) complain about how bad the idlis tasted
    (B) obtain a full refund for his money
    (C) prevent others from making the same mistake he did
    (D) persuade the company to change the wording on their box

Read the passage carefully and answer the questions that follow.

Earth's Temperature

The world is now warmer than at almost any time since the end of the last ice age and, on present trends, will continue to reach a record high for the entire period since the dawn of civilisation, a study has found.

The study published in the journal Science, aims to give a global overview of Earth's temperatures over the past 11,300 years - a relatively balmy period known as the Holocene that began after the last major ice age ended and encompasses all of recorded human civilization.

Their data (compiled by studying such things as ice cores, fossils and ocean sentiment) looked back over a much longer era than previous research, which went back 1,500 years.

Scientists say it is further evidence that modern-day global warming isn't natural, but the result of rising carbon dioxide emissions that have rapidly grown since the Industrial Revolution began roughly 250 years ago. Scientists say that if natural factors were still governing the climate, the Northern Hemisphere would probably be destined to freeze over again in several thousand years. Instead, scientists believe the enormous increase in greenhouse gases caused by industrialization will almost certainly prevent that.

Shaun Marcott, a geologist at Oregon State University, says, "global temperatures are warmer than about 75 percent of anything we've seen over the last 11,000 years or so." The other way to look at that is, 25 percent of the time since the last ice age, it's been warmer than now.

It's taken just 100 years for the average temperature to rise by 1.3 degrees, when it took 5,000 years to do that before. By the end of the century, climate warming models predict an additional increase of 2 to 11.5 degrees, due largely to carbon emissions, the study noted.

26. 'Dawn' in this text means:
    (A) Heat (B) Earth
    (C) Beginning (D) Sunrise

27. 'Balmy' means:
    (A) Warm (B) Cool
    (C) Cold (D) Hot

28. The Earth's temperature has increased quickly since:
    (A) The Holocene
    (B) 1,500 years ago
    (C) The Northern Hemisphere
    (D) The Industrial Revolution

29. 'Prevent' means:
    (A) Complete (B) Stop
    (C) Slow (D) Encourage

30. This article could be described as a ___ look at the future.
    (A) Pessimistic (B) Optimistic
    (C) Egoist (D) Racist

1. Ⓐ Ⓑ Ⓒ Ⓓ	7. Ⓐ Ⓑ Ⓒ Ⓓ	13. Ⓐ Ⓑ Ⓒ Ⓓ	19 Ⓐ Ⓑ Ⓒ Ⓓ	25. Ⓐ Ⓑ Ⓒ Ⓓ
2. Ⓐ Ⓑ Ⓒ Ⓓ	8. Ⓐ Ⓑ Ⓒ Ⓓ	14. Ⓐ Ⓑ Ⓒ Ⓓ	20. Ⓐ Ⓑ Ⓒ Ⓓ	26. Ⓐ Ⓑ Ⓒ Ⓓ
3. Ⓐ Ⓑ Ⓒ Ⓓ	9. Ⓐ Ⓑ Ⓒ Ⓓ	15. Ⓐ Ⓑ Ⓒ Ⓓ	21. Ⓐ Ⓑ Ⓒ Ⓓ	27. Ⓐ Ⓑ Ⓒ Ⓓ
4. Ⓐ Ⓑ Ⓒ Ⓓ	10. Ⓐ Ⓑ Ⓒ Ⓓ	16. Ⓐ Ⓑ Ⓒ Ⓓ	22. Ⓐ Ⓑ Ⓒ Ⓓ	28. Ⓐ Ⓑ Ⓒ Ⓓ
5. Ⓐ Ⓑ Ⓒ Ⓓ	11. Ⓐ Ⓑ Ⓒ Ⓓ	17. Ⓐ Ⓑ Ⓒ Ⓓ	23. Ⓐ Ⓑ Ⓒ Ⓓ	29. Ⓐ Ⓑ Ⓒ Ⓓ
6. Ⓐ Ⓑ Ⓒ Ⓓ	12. Ⓐ Ⓑ Ⓒ Ⓓ	18. Ⓐ Ⓑ Ⓒ Ⓓ	24. Ⓐ Ⓑ Ⓒ Ⓓ	30. Ⓐ Ⓑ Ⓒ Ⓓ

SPOKEN AND WRITTEN EXPRESSION; PUNCTUATIONS

LEARNING OBJECTIVES

➤ Basic concepts of Punctuation
➤ Common Punctuation marks

PRACTICE EXERCISE

I. Choose the sentence which is correctly punctuated.

1. (A) The python caught yesterday measures 21 feet.
   (B) The python, caught yesterday, measures 21 feet.
   (C) The python, caught yesterday measures 21 feet.
   (D) The python caught yesterday, measures 21 feet.

2. (A) My shirt is green, white, and blue.
   (B) My shirt is green, white and blue.
   (C) My shirt is green white, and blue.
   (D) My shirt is green white and blue.

3. (A) Arvind was born on October 18, 2004.
   (B) Arvind was born on October, 18 2004
   (C) Arvind was born on October 18 2004
   (D) Arvind was born on October 18, 2004

4. (A) Steve, the caretaker opened the door for us.
   (B) Steve the caretaker opened the door for us.
   (C) Steve, the caretaker, opened the door for us.
   (D) Steve the caretaker, opened the door for us.

5. (A) The shop, on the corner sells notebooks and paper.
   (B) The shop on the corner sells notebooks, and paper.
   (C) The shop on the corner, sells notebooks and paper.
   (D) The shop on the corner sells notebooks and paper.

6. (A) Look how beautiful the moon is.
   (B) Look how beautiful the Moon is:
   (C) Look! How beautiful the Moon is.
   (D) Look how beautiful, the moon is.

7. (A) What time does the class start?
   (B) What time does the class start
   (C) What time does the class start.
   (D) What time does the class start!

8. (A) I suggest that you read Shakespeares Macbeth.
   (B) I suggest that you read Shakespeare's "Macbeth".
   (C) I suggest that you read shakespeares macbeth.
   (D) I suggest that you read, Shakespeare's Macbeth.

9. (A) Never forget this point: Think before you speak.
   (B) Never forget this point, Think before you speak.

(C) Never forget this point; Think before you speak.
(D) Never forget this point. Think before you speak.

10. (A) There was a knock on the door he went to open it.
(B) There was a knock on the door; he went to open it.
(C) There was a knock on the door, he went to open it.
(D) There was a knock on the door? he went to open it.

11. (A) You are coming aren't you?
(B) You are coming aren't you!
(C) You are coming aren't you.
(D) You are coming, aren't you?

12. (A) Red is my favourite color I like wearing blue sometimes.
(B) Red is my favourite color I like, wearing blue sometimes.
(C) Red is my favourite color, I like wearing blue sometimes.
(D) Red is my favourite color; I like wearing blue sometimes.

13. (A) I love healthy food: nuts, fruits, and vegetables.
(B) I love healthy food nuts, fruits, and vegetables.
(C) I love healthy food nuts fruits and vegetables.
(D) I love healthy, food nuts, fruits, and vegetables.

14. (A) My brothers car is parked in front of the house.
(B) My brother's car is parked in front of the house.
(C) My brothers car, is parked in front of the house.
(D) My brothers car is parked, in front, of the house.

15. (A) I don't sleep well at night I'm always tired during the day.
(B) I don't sleep well at night, I'm always tired, during the day.
(C) I don't sleep well at night. I'm always tired during the day.
(D) I don't sleep well at night; I'm always tired during the day.

16. (A) The weather is hot; humidity is high.
(B) The weather is hot humidity is high.
(C) The weather is hot; humidity is high
(D) The weather is hot humidity is high;

17. (A) He suddenly shouted to me, Look!
(B) He suddenly shouted to me. "Look!"
(C) He suddenly shouted to me, "Look!"
(D) He suddenly shouted to me! "Look!"

18. (A) Your son plays a few games badminton, football and tennis.
(B) Your son plays a few games: badminton football and tennis.
(C) Your son plays a few games. badminton, football and tennis.
(D) Your son plays a few games: badminton, football and tennis.

19. (A) I am going to receive my mother in law from the station.
(B) I am going to receive my mother-in-law from the station.
(C) I am going to receive my mother in law from the station
(D) I am going to receive, my mother in law, from the station.

20. (A) I am on my way to my friends house.
(B) I am on my way to my friend's house.
(C) I am on my way to my friends' house.
(D) I am on my way to my "friends" house.

21. (A) Some women, who were superstitious, did not attend the ceremony.
(B) Some women who were superstitious did not attend the ceremony.
(C) Some women who were superstitious did not attend the ceremony.
(D) Some women, who were superstitious, did not attend, the ceremony.

22. (A) Meet Mark. He is the editor-in-chief.
    (B) Meet Mark. He is the editor-in chief.
    (C) Meet Mark. He is the editorinchief.
    (D) Meet Mark. He is the editor in chief.
23. (A) Do you know how to get there.
    (B) Do you know how to get there!
    (C) Do you know how to get there?
    (D) Do you know how to get there
24. (A) Speech is silver. silence is golden.
    (B) Speech is silver silence is golden.
    (C) Speech is silver-silence is golden.
    (D) Speech is silver; silence is golden.
25. (A) "Listen up everyone," the class monitor yelled.
    (B) Listen up everyone, the class monitor yelled.
    (C) "Listen up everyone, the class monitor yelled."
    (D) "Listen u

HOTS (ACHIEVERS SECTION)

I. Correct the punctuation in following sentences

26. the lady is wearing golden stretch pants green eyelids and a hives shaped wig

27. then lady will dress up to go shopping water the plants empty the dustbin answer the phone read a book and get the letters from the box

28. your father has five items in his bathroom a toothbrush shaving cream a razor a bar of soap and a towel

29. hurling has been the national sport of Ireland

30. we wrote the homonyms too to see sea in our notebooks.

1.	Ⓐ Ⓑ Ⓒ Ⓓ	7.	Ⓐ Ⓑ Ⓒ Ⓓ	13.	Ⓐ Ⓑ Ⓒ Ⓓ	19	Ⓐ Ⓑ Ⓒ Ⓓ	25.	Ⓐ Ⓑ Ⓒ Ⓓ
2.	Ⓐ Ⓑ Ⓒ Ⓓ	8.	Ⓐ Ⓑ Ⓒ Ⓓ	14.	Ⓐ Ⓑ Ⓒ Ⓓ	20.	Ⓐ Ⓑ Ⓒ Ⓓ	26.	Ⓐ Ⓑ Ⓒ Ⓓ
3.	Ⓐ Ⓑ Ⓒ Ⓓ	9.	Ⓐ Ⓑ Ⓒ Ⓓ	15.	Ⓐ Ⓑ Ⓒ Ⓓ	21.	Ⓐ Ⓑ Ⓒ Ⓓ	27.	Ⓐ Ⓑ Ⓒ Ⓓ
4.	Ⓐ Ⓑ Ⓒ Ⓓ	10.	Ⓐ Ⓑ Ⓒ Ⓓ	16.	Ⓐ Ⓑ Ⓒ Ⓓ	22.	Ⓐ Ⓑ Ⓒ Ⓓ	28.	Ⓐ Ⓑ Ⓒ Ⓓ
5.	Ⓐ Ⓑ Ⓒ Ⓓ	11.	Ⓐ Ⓑ Ⓒ Ⓓ	17.	Ⓐ Ⓑ Ⓒ Ⓓ	23.	Ⓐ Ⓑ Ⓒ Ⓓ	29.	Ⓐ Ⓑ Ⓒ Ⓓ
6.	Ⓐ Ⓑ Ⓒ Ⓓ	12.	Ⓐ Ⓑ Ⓒ Ⓓ	18.	Ⓐ Ⓑ Ⓒ Ⓓ	24.	Ⓐ Ⓑ Ⓒ Ⓓ	30.	Ⓐ Ⓑ Ⓒ Ⓓ

MODEL TEST PAPER

PRACTICE EXERCISE

I. Choose the best word/phrase to complete each sentence.

1. The tiger __________ is decreasing rapidly.
   (A) calculation   (B) circulation
   (C) population   (D) education

2. Ram and Kumar have had a fight, they __________ spoken to each other for the last two weeks.
   (A) will be   (B) can't
   (C) aren't   (D) haven't

3. What's all that noise? What's __________?
   (A) occurring   (B) happening
   (C) going   (D) playing

4. What is a doctor's job?
   (A) He promises.   (B) He insists.
   (C) He prescribes.   (D) He proposes.

5. When Steven broke his car's windscreen while playing cricket, his father __________.
   (A) hit the roof   (B) hit the ball
   (C) hit the road   (D) hit the sack

6. Hockey players earn __________ money than cricket players.
   (A) fewer   (B) less
   (C) little   (D) few

7. I don't remember __________ before an exam. My mind goes blank.
   (A) everything   (B) something
   (C) nothing   (D) anything

8. We should drink __________ water during the summer.
   (A) full of   (B) a lot of
   (C) too many   (D) much

9. Sohail doesn't __________ along with his little sister. They are always arguing.
   (A) go   (B) carry
   (C) get   (D) keep

10. When the wildlife experts __________ that the tiger population was decreasing they startedthe 'save the tiger' campaign.
    (A) discovered   (B) unwrapped
    (C) explored   (D) diagnosed

II. How many words are wrongly spelt in the sentences below?

11. The nurce wraped a bandege round his head.
    (A) 1   (B) 2
    (C) 3   (D) None

12. He tried to brake the bad habit but unfortunately all his efforts have been in vein.
    (A) 3   (B) 2
    (C) 1   (D) None

13. One should never loose ones patience.
    (A) 1   (B) 2
    (C) 3   (D) None

III. Choose the best answer to complete each sentence from the options given.

14. __________ by bus is cheaper than by taxi in a city.
    (A) Driving   (B) Riding
    (C) Tripping   (D) Commuting

15. When the tiger roars in the jungle; all the elephants __________.
    (A) howl   (B) growl
    (C) trumpet   (D) scream

16. I'm on holiday, my daily schedule is quite __________ we can arrange to meet any time.
    (A) adjustable   (B) flexible
    (C) elastic   (D) stretchable

17. During the floods the military constructed a temporary floating __________ over the river.
    (A) pontoon bridge (B) flyover
    (C) bridge   (D) draw bridge

18. His father works in a company which was the first to _______ Compact discs (CDs) in the1970s.
    (A) construct   (B) fabricate
    (C) create   (D) invent

19. Let's have a Chinese __________ tonight – I'm not in the mood to cook.
    (A) take away
    (B) take in

20. His father used to work overtime to __________ money for his education.
    (A) gain   (B) win
    (C) raise   (D) achieve

21. In spite of telling him how to do it again and again he made __________ mistake.
    (A) many   (B) yet another
    (C) all   (D) little

22. I'm going to Singapore for __________ day or two.
    (A) some   (B) the
    (C) a   (D) none of these

23. It was raining and I was __________ late for school.
    (A) greatly   (B) by an hour
    (C) entirely   (D) almost

24. Her hair wasn't real. She was wearing a __________.
    (A) hair color   (B) wig
    (C) curls   (D) hair pin

25. What does 'it slipped my mind' mean?
    (A) Forgot to do something
    (B) Just remembered to do something
    (C) Something went passed my head
    (D) Cannot understand anything

26. Ali promised to give her a lift if it __________.
    (A) is rained   (B) will rain
    (C) rained   (D) rains

27. It was very hot. __________, I put on the air conditioner.
    (A) Even though   (B) But
    (C) Even   (D) Even so

28. I __________ you can write so neatly and I can't.
    (A) am hating   (B) hate
    (C) hate that   (D) hate it

29. I have a toy aeroplane __________ a remote control.
    (A) which with   (B) which has
    (C) has   (D) having

30. You should eat some breakfast before you __________ in the morning.
    (A) left   (B) will leave
    (C) had left   (D) leave

31. Wow! These apples are very tasty, and they were __________ ones I could find.
    (A) cheapest   (B) the cheapest
    (C) cheap   (D) the cheap

32. If I __________ press this round button, will it start playing the movie?
    (A) will   (B) __
    (C) could   (D) would

SECTION-II : READING

Read each passage and answer the questions that follow.

Every year large numbers of plastic bottles wash up on the beaches. However, this problem can be solved if the new plan is brought in, as suggested by the scientists. In the new scheme, fishermen will be encouraged to round up plastic bottles with their fishing nets. They can then sell these and cash in on the rising price of old plastic. The recycling centres can then turn toxic waste into packaging. Scientists believe, this scheme will compensate fishermen for the loss of income due to more and more people turning vegetarian. Scientists aim to bring in this scheme soon before the fishermen are forced to sell their boats.

33. What does, 'bottles wash up on the beach' mean?
    (A) Bottles are washed on the beach.
    (B) Bottles arrive on the shore, carried by the waves.
    (C) Beach is washed by the bottles.
    (D) Bottles are left behind by people visiting the beach.

34. Old plastic is made into useful things in a ______________.
    (A) fishing net   (B) science lab
    (C) recycling centre   (D) beach

35. What is the new scheme?
    (A) Fishermen gather plastic bottles and sell them.
    (B) Fishermen encourage scientists to use fishing nets.
    (C) Fishermen are encouraged to make a circle with the nets.
    (D) Fishermen use fishing nets to make around bottle.

36. Which word in the second paragraph means 'changing habits'?
    (A) Compensate   (B) Forced
    (C) Turning   (D) Income

Sharks

There are many types of sharks found in the oceans around the world. Some of them are very big while others are quite small. You need to be scared of some while others are very calm like the Zebra shark. They are small, gentle shark that can be kept in an aquarium with other fish.

You may be surprised to learn that some of the largest species of sharks in the ocean are the nicest ones to encounter. There are 360 different species of sharks in the world. Some of the sharks we should be scared of are e.g. the Great White Sharks. They have attacked more people than any other shark. Their average length is about 12 feet and weighs about 3,000 pounds. Great white sharks are also different from others because they can lift their heads out of the water. Similar to them in length are the Blue sharks. Blue sharks are the fastest swimming sharks and can even leap out of the water and they can eat almost anything and have attacked people too. Tiger sharks too have attacked people but they come second to Great white shark in attacking people. A different type of shark which can swim in salt and fresh water is Bull shark. It comes after the Blue shark in order, for the number of attacks on people.

37. Which shark does not kill fish or people?
    (A) Blue shark   (B) Bull shark
    (C) Zebra shark   (D) Tiger shark

38. In attacking people which shark comes second of all?
    (A) Great white shark (B) Blue shark
    (C) Bull shark   (D) Tiger shark

39. Which shark can jump out of the water?
    (A) Great white shark (B) Blue shark
    (C) Bull shark   (D) Tiger shark

40. Which shark's average length is 12 feet?
    (A) Great white shark (B) Bull shark
    (C) Zebra shark   (D) Tiger shark

SECTION-III :
Spoken and written expression

I. Choose the best response to complete each conversation.

41. Steve : I live in a big city.
    Jill : ______________.
    (A) I live near the park.
    (B) So do I.
    (C) This place is crowded.
    (D) I also.

42. Robin : Have they got a house in the city too?
    Sam : ______________
    (A) Yes, they have.
    (B) Yes, they do.
    (C) Yes, have got.
    (D) Yes, they do have.

43. Imran : Jay has already eaten two burgers, but he is still hungry.
    Sam: Ok, I will give him __________ burger.

(A) some   (B) other
(C) any   (D) another

44. Clair : We both did an equal amount of work, but he was paid more money than I was.
Bob : _______________.
(A) That's average.
(B) That's not enough.
(C) That's funfair.
(D) That's not fair.

45. 'My computer crashed and I lost all my photos.'
(A) 'I don't think I can replace any photos.'
(B) 'I don't think I can restore any photos.'
(C) 'I don't think I can recover any photos.'
(D) 'I don't think I can remake any photos.'

46. Ram: 'You are _______________ hard today.'
Kumar: 'Yes, I have an exam tomorrow.'
(A) studying   (B) staying
(C) to sleep   (D) sleeping

47. Sonia: 'I can't understand what you are saying.'
(A) 'Could you speak slowlier please.'
(B) 'Could you speak more slowly please.'
(C) 'Could you speak down please.'
(D) 'Could you speak low please.'

48. Vikram: 'I was waiting for your call all day yesterday.'
Sonia : 'Sorry, I had a bit of a problem _______________ through.'
(A) phoning
(B) passing
(C) calling
(D) getting

49. What is the indirect speech of the sentence. Ali said, 'I'm working on the science project'.
(A) Ali said that he will be working on the science project.
(B) Ali said that he is working on the science project.
(C) Ali said that he was working on the science project.
(D) Ali said that he had worked on the science project.

50. 'You are probably sleepy, because you _______________.'
(A) are yawning a lot.
(B) went out for lunch.
(C) ate too much chocolates.
(D) watched a movie.

―――――Darken Your Choice with HB Pencil―――――

1.	Ⓐ Ⓑ Ⓒ Ⓓ	11.	Ⓐ Ⓑ Ⓒ Ⓓ	21.	Ⓐ Ⓑ Ⓒ Ⓓ	31	Ⓐ Ⓑ Ⓒ Ⓓ	41.	Ⓐ Ⓑ Ⓒ Ⓓ
2.	Ⓐ Ⓑ Ⓒ Ⓓ	12.	Ⓐ Ⓑ Ⓒ Ⓓ	22.	Ⓐ Ⓑ Ⓒ Ⓓ	32.	Ⓐ Ⓑ Ⓒ Ⓓ	42.	Ⓐ Ⓑ Ⓒ Ⓓ
3.	Ⓐ Ⓑ Ⓒ Ⓓ	13.	Ⓐ Ⓑ Ⓒ Ⓓ	23.	Ⓐ Ⓑ Ⓒ Ⓓ	33.	Ⓐ Ⓑ Ⓒ Ⓓ	43.	Ⓐ Ⓑ Ⓒ Ⓓ
4.	Ⓐ Ⓑ Ⓒ Ⓓ	14.	Ⓐ Ⓑ Ⓒ Ⓓ	24.	Ⓐ Ⓑ Ⓒ Ⓓ	34.	Ⓐ Ⓑ Ⓒ Ⓓ	44.	Ⓐ Ⓑ Ⓒ Ⓓ
5.	Ⓐ Ⓑ Ⓒ Ⓓ	15.	Ⓐ Ⓑ Ⓒ Ⓓ	25.	Ⓐ Ⓑ Ⓒ Ⓓ	35.	Ⓐ Ⓑ Ⓒ Ⓓ	45.	Ⓐ Ⓑ Ⓒ Ⓓ
6.	Ⓐ Ⓑ Ⓒ Ⓓ	16.	Ⓐ Ⓑ Ⓒ Ⓓ	26.	Ⓐ Ⓑ Ⓒ Ⓓ	36.	Ⓐ Ⓑ Ⓒ Ⓓ	46.	Ⓐ Ⓑ Ⓒ Ⓓ
7.	Ⓐ Ⓑ Ⓒ Ⓓ	17.	Ⓐ Ⓑ Ⓒ Ⓓ	27.	Ⓐ Ⓑ Ⓒ Ⓓ	37.	Ⓐ Ⓑ Ⓒ Ⓓ	47.	Ⓐ Ⓑ Ⓒ Ⓓ
8.	Ⓐ Ⓑ Ⓒ Ⓓ	18.	Ⓐ Ⓑ Ⓒ Ⓓ	28.	Ⓐ Ⓑ Ⓒ Ⓓ	38.	Ⓐ Ⓑ Ⓒ Ⓓ	48.	Ⓐ Ⓑ Ⓒ Ⓓ
9.	Ⓐ Ⓑ Ⓒ Ⓓ	19.	Ⓐ Ⓑ Ⓒ Ⓓ	29.	Ⓐ Ⓑ Ⓒ Ⓓ	39.	Ⓐ Ⓑ Ⓒ Ⓓ	49.	Ⓐ Ⓑ Ⓒ Ⓓ
10.	Ⓐ Ⓑ Ⓒ Ⓓ	20.	Ⓐ Ⓑ Ⓒ Ⓓ	30.	Ⓐ Ⓑ Ⓒ Ⓓ	40.	Ⓐ Ⓑ Ⓒ Ⓓ	50.	Ⓐ Ⓑ Ⓒ Ⓓ

HINTS AND SOLUTIONS

1. NOUN

Answer Key

1. (B)	2. (B)	3. (A)	4. (C)	5. (B)	6. (D)	7. (B)	8. (B)	9. (A)	10. (B)
11. (A)	12. (A)	13. (B)	14. (B)	15. (B)					

II									
16. (B)	27. (A)	18. (A)	19. (D)	20. (C)	21. (B)	22. (C)	23. (D)	24. (A)	25. (D)

HOTS (ACHIEVERS SECTION)

26. (D)	27. (A)	28. (D)	29. (D)	30. (D)

2. PRONOUN

Answer Key

1. (A)	2. (D)	3. (B)	4. (A)	5. (A)	6. (D)	7. (B)	8. (B)	9. (C)	10. (C)
11. (A)	12. (C)	13. (C)	14. (A)	15. (A)					

II									
16. (A)	17. (B)	18. (D)	19. (A)	20. (D)	21. (B)	22. (A)	23. (D)	24. (C)	25. (A)

HOTS (ACHIEVERS SECTION)

26. (D)	27. (B)	28. (A)	29. I (B)	II. (C)
III. (C)	IV. (D)			

Answer Key

I

1. (C)	2. (A)	3. (D)	4. (C)	5. (D)	6. (A)	7. (B)	8. (C)	9. (A)	10. (A)

II

11. (B)	12. (B)	13. (C)	14. (C)	15. (A)					

III

16. (A)	17. (B)	18. (D)	19. (B)	20. (C)	21. (A)	22. (D)	23. (D)	24. (B)	25. (A)

HOTS (ACHIEVERS SECTION)

26. (A)	27. (B)	28. (C)		

II

29. (i) make out, (ii) came across, (iii) turn up, (iv) called off.	30. (i) takes after, (ii) sets in, (iii) breaks up, (iv) brought out.

4. ADVERB

Answer Key

I

1. (B)	2. (B)	3. (D)	4. (C)	5. (A)	6. (C)	7. (A)	8. (B)	9. (B)	10. (D)

II

11. (A)	12. (B)	13. (D)	14. (A)	15. (A)	16. (B)	17. (C)	18. (D)	19. (B)	20. (A)
21. (D)	22. (A)								

III

23. (A)	24. (C)	25. (A)							

I				
26. (A)	27. (B)	28. (A)	29. (C)	30. (A)

5. ADJECTIVES

Answer Key

I									
1. (D)	2. (A)	3. (C)	4. (A)	5. (A)					

II									
6. (C)	7. (A)	8. (B)	9. (D)	10. (C)	11. (A)	12. (B)	13. (C)	14. (A)	15. (D)
16. (B)	17. (C)	18. (B)	19. (D)	20. (A)					

III									
21. (B)	22. (A)	23. (C)	24. (D)	25. (D)					

HOTS (ACHIEVERS SECTION)

26. (A)	27. (B)	28. (C)	29. (B)	30. (C)

6. ARTICLES

Answer Key

I									
1. (A)	2. (C)	3. (C)	4. (B)	5. (D)	6. (C)	7. (A)	8. (A)	9. (D)	10. (A)
11. (A)	12. (B)	13. (B)	14. (A)	15. (B)	16. (A)	17. (D)	18. (B)	19. (D)	20. (A)

II									
21. (A)	22. (C)	23. (B)	24. (A)	25. (C)					

26. (D)	27. (D)	28. (C)	29. (C)	30. (B)

7. PREPOSITION

Answer Key

I

1. (D)	2. (A)	3. (B)	4. (A)	5. (D)	6. (B)	7. (A)	8. (A)	9. (B)	10. (C)
11. (A)	12. (D)	13. (B)	14. (C)	15. (B)	16. (D)	17. (C)	18. (B)	19. (D)	20. (A)

II

21. (A)	22. (C)	23. (D)	24. (B)	25. (A)					

HOTS (ACHIEVERS SECTION)

I

26. (C)	27. (C)	28. (B)	29. (A)	30. (A)

8. CONJUNCTIONS

Answer Key

I

1. (D)	2. (A)	3. (C)	4. (B)	5. (D)	6. (A)	7. (A)	8. (C)	9. (B)	10. (D)

II

11. (A)	12. (B)	13. (B)	14. (C)	15. (B)	16. (A)	17. (B)	18. (C)	19. (A)	20. (B)

HOTS (ACHIEVERS SECTION)

21. (A)	22. (C)	23. (A)	24. (B)	25. (D)

Answer Key

I

1. (D)	2. (C)	3. (B)	4. (A)	5. (D)					

II

6. (B)	7. (A)	28. (C)	29. (D)	10. (C)					

III

11. (B)	12. (C)	13. (A)	14. (A)	15. (D)					

IV

16. (A)	17. (B)	18. (C)	19. (B)	20. (D)	21. (C)	22. (B)	23. (A)	24. (A)	25. (D)

HOTS (ACHIEVERS SECTION)

I.

26. Vishal was not living in Kolkata in July last year.
27. Vimal was not talking to Vijay at ten o'clock last night.
28. At four o'clock yesterday we all were not drinking tea.
29. I was not trying to get a taxi at ten o'clock last night.
30. It was not raining in Chennai at five o'clock last evening.

Answer Key

I

1. (A)	2. (A)	3. (A)	4. (B)	5. (C)	6. (A)	7. (C)	8. (B)	9. (A)	10. (B)
11. (A)	12. (B)	13. (C)	14. (A)	15. (B)					

II

16. (A)	17. (B)	18. (B)	19. (B)	20. (A)	21. (C)	22. (B)	23. (B)	24. (B)	25. (C)

I				
26. (D)	27. (C)	28. (A)	29. (C)	30. (A)

11. NARRATION

Answer Key

I									
1. (D)	2. (A)	3. (B)	4. (C)	5. (A)	6. (C)	7. (D)	8. (D)	9. (A)	10. (B)

II									
11. (A)	12. (B)	13. (D)	14. (A)	15. (B)	16. (A)	17. (B)	18. (C)	19. (A)	20. (D)

HOTS (ACHIEVERS SECTION)

I				
21. (A)	22. (A)	23. (D)	24. (A)	25. (B)

II

21. He says, "I am going to Calcutta."
22. He said, "I want a book."
23. Ravi said to his friend, "You may go when you like."
24. The teacher said to me, "You have not done your work well."
25. Suresh said, "I wrote a letter."

12. SYNONYMS AND ANTONYMS

Answer Key

1. (D)	2. (D)	3. (D)	4. (A)	5. (B)	6. (C)	7. (C)	8. (B)	9. (B)	10. (D)
11. (B)	12. (C)	13. (D)	14. (D)	15. (A)	16. (A)	17. (C)	18. (D)	19. (C)	20. (B)
21. (C)	22. (C)	23. (D)	24. (B)	25. (C)					

1. (D)

   Courageous means brave and bold. Thus, fearless is the synonym of courageous

2. (D)

   Watchfulness means vigilant or alert.

3. (D)

   Illicit means not sanctioned by law. Elicit means to draw a response with difficulty hegitimate means legal/lawful.

6. (C)

   Onslaught means' attack'; arrogant means 'full of pride.

7. (C)

   Obvious means 'clear', 'atrocious' means 'cruel', ferocious means full of anger.

8. (B)

   Raja Ram Mohan Roy was the founder of Brahmo Samaj. In other words, he established it.

9. (B)

   When a cyclone affects an area, the people are deprived of their belongings. You then give them money, clothes, food etc. Such gifts to the poor and needy are called alms. Since they are given out of charity (kindness and tolerance), these gifts are also known as charity.

10. (D)

    If you are discomfited by something, it causes you to feel slightly embarrassed or confused. In other words, it, frustrates you.

11. (B)

    Wrath is extreme anger.

12. (C)

    If you abstain from something, you deliberately do not do it. Abstinence, however, is a particular kind of abstaining ?that from alcoholic drink, sex etc., often for health or religious reasons. If you abstain from drinking, you do not get drunk. Abstinence does not refer to "drink" only.

13. (D)

    Your faculties are your physical and mental abilities. We have all been endowed with the faculty of imagination. Most of us, however, kill it through an exercise of constant neglect.

14. (D)

    Filth means dirt, Lewd means characterless. A chaste person does not have sex with anyone or has it only with his or her spouse.

15. (A)

    Imbecility means mental weakness, Insanity means madness. Reverie means day -dreaming.

16. (A)

    Augury is an omen, token, or indication.

17. (C)

    As an adjective, animate simply means "having life". For example: Plants and animals are animate objects. (5) is thus rejected because boisterous means "lively, cheerful". Now, as a verb: If you animate something, you make it lively or more cheerful. Thus you put energy into it. In other words, you energise it. Note: Boisterous is a synonym of the adjective animated.

19. (C)

    Origin means the starting point and remnant is what is left after finishing or distribution.

20. (B)

    Prove means to state that a statement or theory is correct after giving valid and logical reasons while assumption is something which is believed without any proofs or evidence.

21. (C)

    Instantly means something that happens in an instant or very quickly, gradually means to happen step by step.

22. (C)

    Biased teachers are not worthy of respect.

Teachers are expected to be impartial. If not so, they do not deserve respect. In other words, they are undeserving of respect.

23. (D)

Only 76 countries participated in the meet. The rest boycotted it. That is, they refused to participate (take part) in it because they disapproved of it.

24. (B)

Option (A) is rejected because filled is the antonym of empty Hollow should not be confused with empty That which is hollow has a space inside it, as opposed to being solid all the way through. If you fill a hollow cylinder with gas, it still remains hollow, though not empty If ceases to be hollow only when you convert all the space inside into solid.

25. (C)

That which is wild lacks discipline and control. When it is brought under control, it becomes tamed.

HOTS (ACHIEVERS SECTION)

26. (B)	27. (D)	28. (C)	29. (B)	30. (A)

1. (B)

Counsel also means 'legal adviser'.

2. (D)

Quote means repeat something spoken, written by another. These, cite is synonym of quote.

3. (C)

Judicious means having good sense, momentous means most important, pragmatic means practical, treating in a sensible and realistic way.

4. (B)

Having piled a huge total, the Sri Lankan cricket team was in a dominating position. That is, the Sri Lankans were in control of the match (the Independence Cup final). The Pakistani a succumbed to the pressure. That is, they were affected the Sri Lankan domination.

5. (A)

My success is due to my elder brother, who has inspired me at every point. That is, he encouraged me to go ahead with my work. The opposite of encouraged is discouraged.

13. WORD POWER

Answer Key

I				
1. (A)	2. (C)	3. (B)	4. (A)	5. (D)
II				
6. (A)	17. (D)	18. (B)	19. (C)	10. (A)

<table>
<tr><td colspan="5" align="center">III</td></tr>
<tr><td>11. (A)</td><td>12. (C)</td><td>13. (B)</td><td>14. (D)</td><td>15. (A)</td></tr>
<tr><td colspan="5" align="center">IV</td></tr>
<tr><td>16. (B)</td><td>17. (A)</td><td>18. (C)</td><td>19. (A)</td><td>20. (D)</td></tr>
</table>

HOTS (ACHIEVERS SECTION)

<table>
<tr><td colspan="5" align="center">I</td></tr>
<tr><td>21. (D)</td><td>22. (D)</td><td>23. (C)</td><td>24. (C)</td><td>25. (A)</td></tr>
</table>

14. COMPREHENSION

Answer Key

<table>
<tr><td colspan="5" align="center">I</td></tr>
<tr><td>1. (C)</td><td>2. (B)</td><td>3. (A)</td><td>4. (A)</td><td>5. (B)</td></tr>
<tr><td colspan="5" align="center">II</td></tr>
<tr><td>6. (B)</td><td>7. (B)</td><td>8. (C)</td><td>9. (B)</td><td>10. (C)</td></tr>
<tr><td colspan="5" align="center">III</td></tr>
<tr><td>11. (B)</td><td>12. (B)</td><td>13. (C)</td><td>14. (B)</td><td>15. (C)</td></tr>
<tr><td colspan="5" align="center">IV</td></tr>
<tr><td>16. (B)</td><td>17. (C)</td><td>18. (A)</td><td>19. (D)</td><td>20. (B)</td></tr>
<tr><td colspan="5" align="center">V</td></tr>
<tr><td>21. (A)</td><td>22. (D)</td><td>23. (C)</td><td>24. (C)</td><td>25. (B)</td></tr>
</table>

HOTS (ACHIEVERS SECTION)

<table>
<tr><td>26. (C)</td><td>27. (A)</td><td>28. (D)</td><td>29. (B)</td><td>30. (A)</td></tr>
</table>

15. SPOKEN AND WRITTEN EXPRESSION; PUNCTUATIONS

Answer Key

I

1. (B)	2. (B)	3. (A)	4. (C)	5. (D)	6. (C)	7. (A)	8. (B)	9. (A)	10. (B)
11. (D)	12. (D)	13. (A)	14. (B)	15. (D)	16. (A)	17. (C)	18. (D)	19. (B)	20. (B)
21. (A)	22. (A)	23. (C)	24. (D)	25. (A)					

HOTS (ACHIEVERS SECTION)

26. The lady is wearing golden stretch pants, green eyelids and a hives shaped wig.

27. The lady will dress up to go shopping, water the plants, empty the dustbin, answer the phone, read a book and get the letter from the box.

28. Your father has five items in his bathroom – a toothbrush, shaving cream, a razor, a bar of soap and a towel.

29. Hurling has been the national sport of Ireland.

30. We wrote the homonyms too, to see sea in our notebooks.

MODEL TEST PAPER

Answer Key

1. (C)	2. (D)	3. (B)	4. (C)	5. (A)	6. (B)	7. (D)	8. (B)	9. (C)	10. (A)
11. (C)	12. (B)	13. (A)	14. (D)	15. (C)	16. (B)	17. (A)	18. (D)	19. (A)	20. (C)
21. (B)	22. (C)	23. (D)	24. (B)	25. (A)	26. (D)	27. (A)	28. (C)	29. (B)	30. (D)
31. (B)	32. (B)	33. (B)	34. (C)	35. (A)	36. (C)	37. (C)	38. (D)	39. (B)	40. (A)
41. (B)	42. (A)	43. (C)	44. (D)	45. (C)	46. (A)	47. (B)	48. (D)	49. (C)	50. (A)

SAMPLE OMR ANSWER SHEET

1. STUDENT NAME (IN ENGLISH CAPITAL LETTERS ONLY)

Students must write and darken the respective circles completely using HB Pencil only. Othewise their Answer Sheets will not be evaluated.

PERSONAL DETAILS

2. SCHOOL CODE

3. CLASS

4. SECTION

5. ROLL NO.

6. QUESTION PAPER SET

A ○
B ○
C ○
D ○

7. MOBILE NUMBER

8. GENDER

MALE ○
FEMALE ○

9. STREAM
(Only for Class XI and XII Students)

MATHEMATICS ○
BIOLOGY ○
OTHERS ○

MARK YOUR ANSWERS

No.	A	B	C	D	No.	A	B	C	D
1.	Ⓐ	Ⓑ	Ⓒ	Ⓓ	26.	Ⓐ	Ⓑ	Ⓒ	Ⓓ
2.	Ⓐ	Ⓑ	Ⓒ	Ⓓ	27.	Ⓐ	Ⓑ	Ⓒ	Ⓓ
3.	Ⓐ	Ⓑ	Ⓒ	Ⓓ	28.	Ⓐ	Ⓑ	Ⓒ	Ⓓ
4.	Ⓐ	Ⓑ	Ⓒ	Ⓓ	29.	Ⓐ	Ⓑ	Ⓒ	Ⓓ
5.	Ⓐ	Ⓑ	Ⓒ	Ⓓ	30.	Ⓐ	Ⓑ	Ⓒ	Ⓓ
6.	Ⓐ	Ⓑ	Ⓒ	Ⓓ	31.	Ⓐ	Ⓑ	Ⓒ	Ⓓ
7.	Ⓐ	Ⓑ	Ⓒ	Ⓓ	32.	Ⓐ	Ⓑ	Ⓒ	Ⓓ
8.	Ⓐ	Ⓑ	Ⓒ	Ⓓ	33.	Ⓐ	Ⓑ	Ⓒ	Ⓓ
9.	Ⓐ	Ⓑ	Ⓒ	Ⓓ	34.	Ⓐ	Ⓑ	Ⓒ	Ⓓ
10.	Ⓐ	Ⓑ	Ⓒ	Ⓓ	35.	Ⓐ	Ⓑ	Ⓒ	Ⓓ
11.	Ⓐ	Ⓑ	Ⓒ	Ⓓ	36.	Ⓐ	Ⓑ	Ⓒ	Ⓓ
12.	Ⓐ	Ⓑ	Ⓒ	Ⓓ	37.	Ⓐ	Ⓑ	Ⓒ	Ⓓ
13.	Ⓐ	Ⓑ	Ⓒ	Ⓓ	38.	Ⓐ	Ⓑ	Ⓒ	Ⓓ
14.	Ⓐ	Ⓑ	Ⓒ	Ⓓ	39.	Ⓐ	Ⓑ	Ⓒ	Ⓓ
15.	Ⓐ	Ⓑ	Ⓒ	Ⓓ	40.	Ⓐ	Ⓑ	Ⓒ	Ⓓ
16.	Ⓐ	Ⓑ	Ⓒ	Ⓓ	41.	Ⓐ	Ⓑ	Ⓒ	Ⓓ
17.	Ⓐ	Ⓑ	Ⓒ	Ⓓ	42.	Ⓐ	Ⓑ	Ⓒ	Ⓓ
18.	Ⓐ	Ⓑ	Ⓒ	Ⓓ	43.	Ⓐ	Ⓑ	Ⓒ	Ⓓ
19.	Ⓐ	Ⓑ	Ⓒ	Ⓓ	44.	Ⓐ	Ⓑ	Ⓒ	Ⓓ
20.	Ⓐ	Ⓑ	Ⓒ	Ⓓ	45.	Ⓐ	Ⓑ	Ⓒ	Ⓓ
21.	Ⓐ	Ⓑ	Ⓒ	Ⓓ	46.	Ⓐ	Ⓑ	Ⓒ	Ⓓ
22.	Ⓐ	Ⓑ	Ⓒ	Ⓓ	47.	Ⓐ	Ⓑ	Ⓒ	Ⓓ
23.	Ⓐ	Ⓑ	Ⓒ	Ⓓ	48.	Ⓐ	Ⓑ	Ⓒ	Ⓓ
24.	Ⓐ	Ⓑ	Ⓒ	Ⓓ	49.	Ⓐ	Ⓑ	Ⓒ	Ⓓ
25.	Ⓐ	Ⓑ	Ⓒ	Ⓓ	50.	Ⓐ	Ⓑ	Ⓒ	Ⓓ

Signature of the Student & Date of Examination

Signature of the Invigilator & Date of Examination